LEARNING FACTORS CHANGE ORGANIZATIONAL BEHAVIOR

JOHN LOK

Contents

Contents

Preface

Introduction

Organizational behavior is important to influence any organizational success. If the organization can build good and efficient organizational culture. Then it can help this organization to build good organizational behavior. Consuquently, employees can achieve the best performance. I shall attempt to explain some cases how to apply strategies to help organizations to build good organizational behaviors. Readers can learn useul organizational behavioral knowledge.

Prologue

Table of content

CHAPTER I

learning organizational culture

1. Describe the culture or cultures at Hill wood Medical Centre ? Are these subcultures?

Organizational cultures and subcultures will influence Hill wood Medical Centre organizational performance and commitments. The subcultures may take precedence over the organizational culture for individual employees and thus gain their commitment. Hill wood medical centre can therefore focus on the relationships of both organizational culture and subcultures to satisfy staffs need to serve patients in happy work environment.

Organizational culture includes leadership style and job satisfactory measurement.

Hence, employees' commitment was examined in relation to the level of consent to and conflict with managerial strategy. Although, managerial strategy is not the same as leadership, the attributes and skills required in leadership could be seen as an essential part of managerial strategy. Organization culture(s) has (have) a causal modelling approach to examine the determinants of organizational commitment and labour turnover.

Organization culture(s) can include a variety of variables , e.g. age, pre-employment expectations, perceived job characteristics and the consideration of leadership style, which all influence organizational commitment indirectly via effects on job satisfaction.

I supposed that Hill Wood Medical Centre existed relationship of organizational culture and subcultures to influence staffs feel satisfactory and commitment. Also of interest is the relationship of these variables with leadership style, job satisfaction and subject characteristics, such as age, level of education to its staffs in this hospital.

In Hill Wood Medical Centre organization, its organizational culture was the hospital cultures and subcultures which refer to the culture of the wards or work units or operation rooms to every department staff commitments refer to nurses team and medical service chief medical officer team and surgeons team and administrative department etc their different departments' individual staff's commitments.

There is a culture relationship between this medical centre organization commitments and it was measured with administration department and operating rooms and wards department etc different departments' subcultures as well as surgeons and nurses and doctors and administration staffs etc different teams' subcultures.

More specifically, it is expected that such as Hill Wood Medical Centre organizational culture could be more supportive and innovative to its different departments, such as wards and surgeons operating rooms and administrative office etc different departments subcultures.

Thus, I believe there is a strong relationship between this medical centre

organizational cultures and subcultures and commitment and characteristics of

this organizational overall culture, such as corporate values and beliefs commitments

and performance to Hill Wood Medical Centre organization.

However, I think this medical centre's bureaucratic work practices organizational

cultures often result in negative employee commitment due to its supportive work

environment could not result in greater commitment and involvement among employees.

For example, these different departments needed to met Sharon Lawson,

administrator of Hill Wood Medical Centre to discuss how to solve their departments

problems in their meetings in that day, but Sharon Lawson could not had any

suggestions in these meeting in that day. It seemed that this medical centre

had negative culture and subcultures to get negative results due to who needed

to spend time to wait Sharon to meet them and the administrator could not give any suggestions

to solve their department problems on that day. Such as Holly from state health department told

Sharon the general inspection needed to be improved, e.g. kitchen needed

cleanliness and inspectors felt this medical centre needed to allow patients access to drug supplies, but this state health department representative

had requested inspection before six months and Helen controller asked Sharon about

the new computer hardware who requested six months ago and Helen told

Sharon who needed it now for billing efficiency to office use, but

Sharon decided to make request to board for computer hardware purchase

next meeting and some surgeons were drunk to work in operating rooms,

who caused danger to patient's life to cause some patients complained

these surgeons, but Sharon did not solve whose complaints at that day immediately and

medical staffs were discussing why the medical centre had not purchased

one upgraded piece of standard diagnostic equipment used in body scanning $700,000 cost,

but Sharon had not enquired whose reasons clearly to decide to buy the equipment next year,

but doctors did not understand why Sharon could not purchased this year.

Then the nurses agreed to give Sharon a week to investigate the situation

and attempted to resolve it and a meeting was scheduled for next week to review

the situation. Finally the medical centre's attorney needed to wait for twenty minutes

to discuss about what steps were to be taken to solve with surgeons, Dr Chambers

who was complained about drunk wine work in surgeon operating rooms issue, but

Sharon had no more time to meet whom to discuss on that day. Hence, it seemed that this medical centre had not good culture and subcultures in its organization, such as

Sharon had not enough time arrangement to meet them to discuss their departments'

problems on the same day. It seemed that Hill Wood Medical Centre had no good

organizational culture and subcultures to cause staffs conflicts and administration

department also wasted much time to handle departments' meetings only. If Hill

Wood Medical centre culture and subcultures could be changes, such as every

department could attempt to discuss how to solve their problems before who met the

administrator . Then I believe that who could give reasons or ideas to support

their view point to persuade Sharon made final decision to shorten their meeting time.

Hence, this medical centre seemed that it's subcultures and culture were negative.

I supposed that it's nurses team subcultures tended to identify more cooperation closely

with different teams, such as surgeons operating rooms team, doctors team, wards team

etc departments to compare the administration department. It meant nurses teams' subcultures

needed often exhibit greater loyalty and commitment to these departments in the Hill wood

Medical Centre organization. Thus, it seemed that it needed better subcultures in nurses teams to

share different departments' job to reduce staffs conflicts to serve patients satisfactory.

However, Hill Wood Medical Centre organizational culture and subcultures could influence

staffs' job satisfaction and commitment positively or negatively due to this medical centre

cultural variables could influence their feelings , such as the amount of reward,

flexibility of work schedule and balance of work and home life etc.

Hence, Hill Wood Medical Centre culture could cause those intrinsic factors to influence

every units staffs' feelings of job satisfaction. In relation to educational level and organizational

commitment, it seemed that educational level was negatively relative to this Hill Wood Medical

centre, such as it could permit surgeons were drunk to work in operating rooms often, it was

danger to every patient life during surgeons were drunk to work

.

Hill Wood Medical Centre overall culture was from low to top level communication channel and

bureaucratic work organizational culture was often in negative employee commitment, such as

all departments needed to wait the administrator to arrange meeting time to solve

their departments problems in the same day. However, much decisions could not get

solutions from the administrator.

It seemed that this Hill Wood Medical Centre's bureaucratic organization cultures and

subcultures caused Sharon had arranged more meetings on that day to influence who had not

enough time to do their departments' duties on that day efficiently due to who only concentrated on handling meetings issues on that day.

I think Sharon Lawson who did not know how to arrange what kinds of job duties and meetings

which were more important which ought to handle on that day or what kinds of job duties

and meetings which were not more important to handle on the same day.

Hence, who could not get any discussion result in these meetings on that day due to Sharon,

administrator had not enough time to negotiate their departments to solve problems

successfully in meetings.

In conclusion, this medical centre organizational cultures and subcultures seemed that which

were not positive to staffs' commitments and job satisfaction. Such as its different

departments needed to spend much time to wait administrator to arrange meetings to discuss

their problems, but who did not make any decisions in their meetings. The administrator would

influence different departments overall work efficiency and effectiveness to be poor.

So, it ought need to change its organization culture and subcultures to raise its

different departments' efficiency and effectiveness as soon as possible.

2. How would you recommend that Sharon administrator measure

effectiveness at Hill wood Medical Centre?

The medical centre performance effective evaluation meant to measure whether the degree to

its overall organization was improving or deteriorating. The measurement combines quantitative and qualitative analysis and efficiency trend to get the degree of effective result. On the

quantitative analyses measurement, e.g. medical errors occurrence rates ; patients

medical treatment health rates. On the qualitative analysis measurement, e.g.

acquiring executives who communicated a culture of quality through personal supportive polities

and investment of resources, such as the degree of diagnostic equipments effectiveness,

the degree of staff quality improvement and the degree of health information technological

effectiveness and the degree of every patient's service satisfaction etc.

Performance measurement effectiveness is well established throughout medical and health care

industry, of which include the core areas of finance, operations, clinical care and information

technology services as below:

Finance is an organization often measures the efficiency of its accounts receivable, i.e. timely

collection of payment for services rendered, such as this Hill Wood medical centre can collect

how much payment for services from patients per week and it earns how much profit or loss

per week.

Operating is an organization needs the lengths of time to take for a patient to receive an

appointment in the practice or measures individual patient whose satisfaction with the

care received, such as the satisfactory degree of Hill Wood Medical Centre every patient how who feel to every doctor, physician, surgeon and nurse whose service performance

and personal attitude to whom.

Clinical care is an organization measures how often care is delivered in accordance with

evidence based guidelines or how effective that care is in improving every patient outcome,

such as whether Hill Wood medical centre had how many doctor and surgeon and physician and

nurse numbers who could treat every patient to be health to satisfy who don't feel sick or

hurt again after who left this hospital.

Information technology is an organization widely integrated into health care settings to support

for performance measurement, such as whether Hill Wood medical centre needed to buy

how many diagnostic equipments to use to body scanning for surgeons or needed to buy

how many computers to office to use to achieve the best performance.

This Hill Wood medical centre needed these processes to measure its quantified numbers to a

health care service provided to on behalf of or by a patient that was needed on scientific evidence

of efficiency or effectiveness, so it could quantify a specific system, e.g. getting a test done or a

service performed and it's outcome could measure to quantify every patient's health status resulting

from its nurses and doctors and surgeons and physicians whose health care. Thus, in the clinical area, Hill Wood medical centre could measure every patient outcome to compare to every care standard, such as every patient's test value to measure effectiveness. Measurement effectiveness is central to the concept of this Hill Wood medical centre quality improvement, it provides a mean to define what medical centres or hospitals actually do and to compare that with the original targets in order to identify opportunities for improvement.

On clinical care and operational measure aspect:

Hill Wood medical centre ought to establish standardized and systematic procedures for problem solving to able to test and implement major practice changes. Such as clinical guidelines or care maps for specific conditions or procedures, department specific quality plans with short and long term goals, improved educational and training materials for clinical staff error reduction, hand washing and infection prevention, education materials for patients regarding full prevention, information technology that reduced medication errors and improved data collection etc these changes. To decide whether how much change criteria it ought need to change it's measurement effectiveness was depending on the nature of the change and the rate of acceptance and adoption of staff. It aimed to resistance to change in culture from surgeons and physicians and nurses and doctors; measured how much limited resources were available to use or maintain quality related equipment investment, such as office equipments or operational rooms diagnostic equipments of numbers as well as

whether how to make the patient complaint numbers to be reduced to

achieve zero tolerance to any staffs as well as whether departmental

quality plans could achieve special goals effectiveness measurement

as well as whether training could be achieve continuous quality improvement to staffs measure

effectiveness as well as organizational structure change could be raised staffs service

performance efficiently, such as whether creation was needed

on service quality and addition staff and responsibilities were needed for quality improvement

as well as whether patient care redesign and more training was needed for aides and

multi disciplinary leadership teams change.

Establishing organizational culture and subcultures of service quality measurement effectiveness

aspect as below:

. Setting how long time to achieve short term and long term attainable goals and celebrated

successes to individual staff and individual units involved in reaching their goals.

. Keeping the individual unit staff involved in problem identification and problem solving

time spending. It aimed to raise everyone to feel much valuing expecting all to participate

to solve any problems in the most shorten time.

On finance and information technology measure effective aspect:

Effective organizational culture and subculture change could encourage every unit leader and peers to be patient, but recognized that changing took time and continuing to keep quality

improvement to measure whether it needed how much time to balance quality and financial

goals and considering investments, such as how many equipment numbers were needed to buy

to provide to office and operational room units to use to raise office productive efficiency

and effectiveness as well as operational rooms service efficiency and effectiveness to measure to

achieve quality improvement from a short and long term perspective to this Hill Wood

medical centre. It aimed to evaluate whether new policies were bringing equipment into

operating rooms or office to use was needed or was not needed .

I recommend Sharon, administrator needed to indicate these qualitative performance

effectiveness measurement questions included:

.What barriers did this medical centre face in implementing the strategies or achieving success?

.Did it overcome those obstacles and if so, how?

In conclusion, to measure effectiveness of this medical centre whether how it could achieve

quality improvement for success. I recommend Sharon, administrator needed to consider what

should be the indicators to include implementation of aggressive quality targets for performance

indicators as well as how to decide tightening of recruitment and standards and enhanced respect

for all staffs in enhancement of quality improvement processes to shorten time to solve problems in efficient manner and hoped to decide new investments in quality related information technology

combined with the number of staffs input numbers efficiently and effectively.

Thus, the four core areas of performance measurement was one quality improvement models

of high performing effective measurement to Hill Wood Medical Centre.

3. What do you think some of the effectiveness criteria might be?

I think some outcomes of effectiveness criteria to this Hill Wood medical centre, it

might be the practice changes appeared to have resulted in improved outcomes for patients. In

addition to major improvements in the combination quality measures which based on morality,

morbidity and complication rates, such as below:

Process/ operations effectiveness criteria: faster receipt of test result, faster patient flow, easier

and more efficient data sharing and recording, fewer medication errors. So, I think it could measure

the doctors and nurses and surgeons and physicians who serve to every patient's performance whether

what effectiveness criteria to these staffs from their every serving patients' satisfactory level.

Health related effectiveness criteria: calculate the reductions in morality rates, e.g.

the surgeon reducing numbers were drunk to work in operational rooms every month

and the patient health numbers every month.

Work environment and reputation effectiveness criteria: increase in patients satisfaction and staff satisfaction numbers and morale improved status numbers every month in this medical centre.

If it could increase the numbers of patients satisfaction and staff satisfaction and morale improved

status numbers, it would have greater ability to improve service quality to surgeons and doctors

and nurses in this medical centre.

Bottom line effectiveness criteria: the effective measurement of decreasing or increasing costs

per medical centre units and length of stay for certain conditions and increased or

decreased patients admission numbers and market share numbers every month.

I think it lacked enough equipments for office to use and diagnostic equipments

numbers were needed to be upgraded to use in body scanning because

the departments leaders needed to met to Sharon, administrator to permit to buy those

equipments urgently. It seemed this medical centre service effectiveness criteria would

be poor due to there was not enough equipments to provide to these units to use possibly.

Hence, if this medical centre could raised the quantitative and qualitative effectiveness

criteria as above, it would change positive outcomes to motivate these units doctors,

surgeons, nurses, physicians and administrative individual team leaders and their colleagues

to strengthen the service quality improvement process to this Hill Wood medical centre.

However, I think this Hill Wood medical centre performance was poor from the above

effectiveness criteria analysis. Performance must be defined in relative to explicit goals
reflecting the values of various stakeholders. This medical centre internal stakeholders were
such as patients, doctors, nurses, surgeons, physicians etc and external stakeholders were
patients, debtors, banks, Government shareholders etc. This medical
centre performance might be defined according to the achievement of specific targets of
either clinic to patient services or internal departmental operations. Targets might relate to
traditional hospital functions, such as health treatment, care and rehabilitation
as well as administration, ambulatory patient delivered services and health care networks.

Following this medical centre evidences which indicated the poor performance of effectiveness
criteria, such as Sharon, administrator lacked enough time to meet some department leaders to
help them to solve problems successfully on that day, so it caused who needed to make another
meetings to discuss their problems again. It seemed the administrator wasted their time to
do other important duties on that day efficiently and effectively. I think Sharon, administrator
was not one effective administrator in this medical centre. If who could not change whose management
attitude to co-operate with other department managers(leaders), then who could cause poor subcultures
to different departments to build to this medical centre overall organization culture
and who also influenced other department performed ineffective and inefficient results due to

Sharon, administrator who did not know how to arrange time to meet them everyone efficiently.

In conclusion, I think if this medical centre hoped to reduce doctors and nurses and surgeons and

physicians and administrations etc staffs frequently conflict and maximized work effectiveness of

its departments. Sharon administrator had responsibility to change whose personal work attitude

to adapt their subcultures to co-operate with different departments. Otherwise, this medical centre

would not be maximize effectiveness and would increase staffs conflicts to cause staff turnover

numbers to be increased seriously.

CHAPTER II

Learning How to Solve Organizational Problems

1. Identify the basic problems at KBTZ

KBTZ was a large television station in United States. It was one of the largest revenue producers in its entertainment market and employed more than 180 staffs and it was as the local television leader in the use of sophisticated electronic equipment. The station's physical plant was planned to accommodate the new equipment and to boost its image at the leader in the entertainment market.

However, its organization development caused much problems to need to solve. On the one hand, due to external pressure to cause organization change, such as entertainment market competition needed to have high technological new equipments to purchase to provide to different departments to use, e.g. cameras, films etc equipment. Hence, different department staffs needed to learn how to use these equipments to raise productive performance quality. On the other hand, due to internal pressure to cause organizational change, such as reducing aspiration performance factor was caused poorly in KNTZ organization, which meant gaps was occurred between what an individual, unit or organization wanted to achieve and what it was actually achieving in KTZ organization.

Due to KBTZ television station's operational department ,engineering department, programming department, sales department, news department etc departments which every department individual staff, work group, division or overall KBTZ organization was not meeting its own expectations to adopt KBTZ new organization changes as well as television programming needed new productive tactics to change new strategies and processes often caused follow poor performing individual staffs, units and KBTZ whole organization, which might reduce aspiration levels instead of making changes sufficient to increase performance. Because KBTZ large television station often compared itself with other television stations in the entertainment industry , when comparisons with similar others suggested that better performance was possible. However, KBTZ staffs could not adopt organizational change development suddenly, so it caused many different departments felt difficult co-operation together in KBTZ television station organization.

In fact, American television station entertainment industry was encountered by life cycle forces, it meant the natural and predictable pressures that built as to KBTZ television station organization grew and that KBTZ television station must hope to continue growing.

Hence, KBTZ television station was at elaboration stage, it meant KBTZ needed for balance, focused on efficiency and innovation, formal procedures existed and empowered low level managers and associates in its organization if KBTZ still wanted to keep its large television station position in United States.

However, KBTZ 's large television station's physical plant planned to accommodate
the new advances equipment to provide different departments staffs to use and to boost its image
as the leader in the United States entertainment market. It would cause its staffs feel difficult to
adapt to adjust efficient and effective co-operation between departments due to it's planning
change caused a process involving deliberate efforts to move KBTZ television station within its
organization undesirable state to a new and more desirable state during KBTZ 's organization
development was carrying on. Hence, due to its organization development change it would cause
these basic problems at KBTZ organization as below:

As I was the KBTZ consultant to meet with Valerie Diaz, president and general manager, who
explained the key problem as:
The first problem was the high stress to which KBTZ 's manager and associates who felt about time
deadlines in television problem, e.g. when it's precisely six o'clock , KBTZ news department staffs
must be on the air with the news. All of the news material, local reporting, news,
interviews must be processed, edited and ready to go at six o'clock.
This news department staffs felt difficult, due to who could not have any half prepared material
extended deadlines to cause lose the KBTZ 's audiences. This situation caused a great deal of
conflict and turnover increased, such as a number of well qualified and motivated employees were

leaving KBTZ television station. The news department's employee turnover was about 35% which

was too high as well as KBTZ also had trouble hiring qualified people who fit their culture and

these new qualified staffs feel difficult to co-operate with KBTZ staffs to cause conflict. It

seemed to be team conflict problem.

The second problem was that business manager felt difficult to manage different departments, due to

who previously worked in sales and in the general manager's office, but who lacked management

training and this was whose first managerial position to help in managing whose departments.

It seemed to be personal difficult management problem.

The third problem seemed the news department and business office and programming

department indicated who felt the new director who lacked leadership ability to manage any

departments, such as new department managers and associates felt extreme dissatisfaction

with the department head, new director who had very negative attitudes toward their overall

work environment , new director lacked leadership ability to let news department managers and

associates communicate easily. Moreover, news department associates also complained of very

low reward, including pay, promotion opportunities and managerial praise and who also

complained of constant criticism, which was the only form of managerial feedback on

performance. Hence, it implied the new director did not attempt to solve any departments staffs difficulties to adopt new organization change to cause their dissatisfaction and conflict and

complaints occurrence to whom. It seemed to be new director personal leadership problem and

news departments staffs team communication and individual dissatisfaction problems.

The fourth problem was operations department manager who complained another departments,

such as news department staffs, who were confused all of the time and engineering groups,

staffs were lazy and who did like cooperation to influence operational department

performed ineffectively, due to these groups needed to co-operate to work together.

So operations manager suggested me (KBTZ 's consultant) dismissed chief engineer and

shaped up (reorganized) the news groups and the engineers groups . It seemed to be

difficult co-operation occurred between operations department and engineering and news both

departments problem.

The fifth problem was chief engineers who complained the unreasonableness of certain

people in other departments. For example, the difficulty indicated that whose team engineers

could not immediately repair some malfunctioning equipment in their area and it could

take several hours just to determine the cause of the failure. It seemed that engineer department

lacked enough engineers and equipments were provided to them to work from operational

department . It caused team conflict problem.

The sixth problem was the program director complained the station was missing a lot of

opportunities in other areas, e.g. news and sales, the chief engineer was incompetent and

operations managers were difficult to motivate low level managers to make any decisions or

took any responsibilities . It seemed the program director who felt dissatisfactory to other

departments personal performance problem.

The seventh problem was the promotion manger who expected a little training to provide in how

to deal with people, innovation and communication problems. It seemed that promotion manager

felt difficult to adopt new organization change problem.

The eighth problem was sales department representatives complained who ought to increase

salaries due to whose good sale performance. It seemed that sales representatives‘

dissatisfactory problem.

Finally, the business office and programming department also made one survey to indicate

individuals in these departments to have generally positive attitude, such as job satisfaction, but

who had two important negative attitude in whose working environment.

In general, these low and middle level staffs whose negative attitude of task environment major

problem indicated who thought that whose department heads and the general manager

could handle downward communication better , it meant that the middle and low level staffs felt the top level managers lacked effective communication to them as well as these were

several comments about being underpaid relative to other station employees.

Although, the survey indicated the managers and associates whose high

satisfaction, but who also believed that the negative factors led them to be poorly motivated.

Such as some low and middle level associates reported that who were not sure who was

top level immediate manager , since both the assignments editor and the assistant news director

gave them assignments. It seemed that who lacked communication between departments to

influence who did not know who had actual authority to give job to them to do.

It would cause difficult to co-operation to finish every job between department. If the assignments

needed to finish urgently, who would influence any news, entertainment programmes could

not been finished before the time deadlines. It seemed to be team communication problem.

The another problem was that, some low and middle level associates also reported that

creativity (thought to be important in the jobs) was discouraged by the director's highly

authority management and structured styled as well as new director personal work attitude

was not good style. It seemed that this new director had unsuitable personal management skill to

lead this KBTZ different departments to follow whose guidelines to finish their jobs daily, to cause these departments ' staffs felt dissatisfactory to this new director's personal work attitude . It

seemed that this was new director's personal management attitude problem.

Moreover, this business office and programming department's survey also indicated these

departments existed these problems in KBTZ television station organization.

Firstly, although most of operation department associates were satisfied with their jobs and

reported pride in their departments and only some associates felt satisfactory about their

operations department manager (head). All other some associates tended to feel overworked

(reported a 74 hours workweek) and thought the department head expected too much and who

also thought who were underpaid relative to their task demands and criticized managerial

feedbacks on their performance and the department head never prised position performance and who

only regarded them for poor performance and who also reported concern over the conflict

with engineering group , but who believed operations and engineering department conflict,

whose departments' leaders (managers) should be resolved.

It seemed that this operations departments manager could not manage some departments staffs

to work in normal hours to cause them to feel unhappy to work and they also felt underpayment

and unreasonable feedback on the performance problem.

Anyway, the engineering department many associates were very dissatisfied with whose jobs and who had conflict to operational department and who also believed engineering department head

did not support them and who lacked department meetings to receive feedback on their

performance from the chief engineer. It seemed that this engineering department's chief

engineer who performed more poor to compare to operations department manager to cause

many associates felt dissatisfactory to him.

Otherwise, the survey indicated that only promotion department associates had positive attitudes

and their job satisfaction were high and everyone viewed their task environment positively

and who had only few negative attitudes were primarily directed toward the ineffectiveness of

the news department . It seemed that promotion department had none any problems, so its

associates could criticize the another news department ineffectiveness result confidently.

Finally, the sales department's colleagues could not responded to the survey to indicate

whether what kinds of problems who felt .Due to sale department head was the KBTZ

television station manager's son family relationship , so who could not respond to complete

this survey whether whose feelings to this sales department manager was

satisfactory or was not satisfactory to him, it would cause who lost their job if who

responded whose actual feelings to me (consultant) to know at that day possibly.

2. Which organization development techniques should I consider using and why?

As I was KBTZ television station consultant, I should apply these organization development techniques to solve this company problems.

Organizational development techniques included relationship techniques, such as T-group training, team building, survey as well as structural technique, such as management by objective and supplemental organizational processes.

The news department problem, such as high stress to this department managers and associates.

It was respect to time deadlines in television problem. The department's staffs must be on the air with the news. All of the news material , local reporting , news , interviews must be processed, edited and ready to go at six o'clock. So, this news department staffs often worried about extended deadlines or who only half prepared material or who lost the audience, it caused conflict and a number of well qualified and motivated employees would leave this KBTZ television station organization and KBTZ also felt trouble hiring new qualified people could adapt KBTZ organization's culture to help KBTZ organization to raise competition in this USA entertainment market. On the other hand, due to news department staffs who were confused all of the time, so it also caused operations department manager who felt difficult co-operation with to cause operations department and news department would be often conflicts about news department extended time deadline issue.

Even, program department director also complained the station was missing a lot of opportunities in other areas, e.g. news and sales.

I should use organization development technology, relationship technique T-group training to solve

this news and operation departments cooperation problem, which meant news department would

implement group exercises in which individual focused on their action, how

others perceived their actions and how others generally reacted to them, so participants often

learnt about unintended. Hence, this news department managers and associates who could

divided several groups, it aimed to focus on their individual action, e.g. local reporting group,

news report group, interviews group, news material preparing group. So, these every

group members (staffs) who could perceived whose individual group action and reacted to

another group individual member action, such as news material preparing group individual

member could focus on gathering news material preparing job duties, then who could gave

news material to news report group individual member to prepare to analyse materials to prepare to report.

Another interviews group individual to prepare how much time needed and what places

should be choose and who to be interviewed to prepare every day different news to let

audience to watch six o'clock news programs in television every day. Then, who could

gave local reporting group individual member to analyze their every individual interviewing

record to produce every local reporting. Thus, T-group training benefit was that participants, such as KBTZ news department's material group individual member, local reporting group

individual member, news production group individual member, interviewed group individual

member who could often learnt about why unintended negative consequences were caused of

certain types of any group individual member's behaviour to cause to extend time deadlines or

to cause only extend time deadlines or to cause only half prepared material due to very few time

was enough to prepare precisely at six o' clock to ready to go before this news department all groups must be

processed to edit. Hence, group member which needed to finish whose identified group job, e.g.

interview group members who only needed to focus on carry on training how to make date

and time appointment to meet individual in the beginning to till to how to prepare what kinds of

interview questions would enquire and every interview was planned which needed how long time

to finish. Hence, such as interview group individual member could review whose every interview

progress to aim to achieve to shorten time to perform the better news programs quality to provide

to television audients to watch at everyday six o'clock news time. Hence, the news department's

every group member could give chance to enquire survey feedback from every team leader (manager)

to review their everyday news job to investigate whether whose group performance would

cause unintended negative consequences to influence other group performance to be poor, such as

investigating the day's news extended causing was due to the day interview group's individual member who could not organize overall interview procedure to arrange time to finish effectively

or other group's individual member to cause. Hence, relationship technique T-group training method

could review whether which group(s) to cause the day news extended deadlines or found whether

which group(s) caused overall team which could not prepare all material to finish the day news

watching at six o'clock . It was one fair method to measure whether which group staffs were qualified

people or whether which group staffs were not qualified people to co-operate in this news department.

Other problem was about business department head, business manager seemed that who lacked

management training to prepare to do this position, such as who previously worked to do this

position, such as who previously worked in sales and in the general manager's office only.

Hence, who must need to provide training to prepare to know how to manage KBTZ 's television

station organization different departments, such as news department, sales department, operations

department, engineering department, program department, promotion department efficiently.

As I was KBTZ 's consultant , I felt KBTZ could provide relationship technique of survey method

to assist whom. If every departments could get survey, then this business manager could obtain

enough dates to meet all units to discuss problems easily. Then, when who collected all departments'

problems from this survey, KBTZ could use structural technique of management by objectives method to assist him (business manager), it meant a management process in which individuals

(different group members) negotiated whose group daily task objectives, such as engineer group

member could negotiate how much equipments who needed to repair urgently and how many

equipments who could repair and gave reasons why who could not repair some equipments in

that day.

All departments might have task objectives to measure whose every group members

performance to revise what factors caused whose performance to be poor in order to correct

to achieve every department's group member could raise work efficiently. Thus, this management

process needed spend much time to revise every department's group individual negotiate task. For

example, the business manager needed to meet engineering group leader (chief engineer) and

members(engineers and technicians) to discuss whether how many equipments who needed to

repair and whether how many equipments who needed to repair and whether how many equipments

who felt who had no much time to repair this week, then next week, this business manager would

enquire these engineers to revise whether what reasons occurred to cause who could not repair

all machines last week. As this engineer department individual member technician who had

negotiated task objectives to let whose chief engineer and engineering manager to know

whether who felt that who could finish task to repair how many machines every week, then they could meet to attempt to explain what factors caused them could not repair all equipments

further week. Hence, this business manager could used the same management by objectives

structural technique method, such as every department individual member needed to negotiate task objective to

finish every week, then who needed to meet whose department manager to revise what factors influenced their

work efficiency, e.g. news department material group could meet to discuss task objective about

how much time and how many staffs who needed to prepare to gather any related material

to report this week ; interview group could meet to discuss task objective about how much time and

how many staffs who needed to prepare to organize any effective interview procedure to prepare

individual interview this week ; news edited group could meet to discuss task objective about

how much time and how many staffs who needed to be edit for daily news this week. Thus, this

business manager could know all department's every group individual task objectives per week

clearly, then who could meet them to attempt to find whether what factors which caused any

department's group individual member who could not achieve whose last week objectives

efficiently and effectively.

The new director seemed have unsuitable personal management style to lead whose different

departments to work together to cause their dissatisfaction to him in this KBTZ television

station organization. For example, the news department felt this new director lacked leadership ability to led news department managers and associates communicate easily. Moreover, news

department associates also complained of very low reward, including pay, promotion opportunities and

managerial praise and who also complained of constant criticism , which was the only form of

managerial feedback on performance. Hence, it implied the new director did not attempt to solve

any departments staffs difficulties to adopt new organization development change to cause their

dissatisfaction and conflicts and complaints occurrence to whom.

I should suggest this new director as a leader who needed to find method to help different

department leader(manager) to lead whose associates to feel this KBTZ organization must

earn more beyond the past by providing a rationale for change currently and let them to feel

guilt and poor anxiety about this KBTZ organization chose not to change and create a sense

of psychological safety to them to concern the change, such as news department associates who

complain of low reward, including low promotion opportunities and managerial praise and who

also complained of constant criticism feedback on performance. It seemed that who would also

complain about low reward, low promotion opportunities and managerial praise and unfair

feedback on performance to this new director , even who had good personal managerial style to

lead all departments to work. A reason was why these departments, such as news department colleagues

complained as above issues because who felt the new director could not adopt to work due to KBTZ sudden change to cause who should be de-commit and dissatisfactory form the status. Hence, this

new director needed to let who to know KBTZ organization would cause poor anxiety and guilt to

them in the future if KBTZ organization did not change at this moment as well as this new director

might create of psychological discomfort to these departments to let them to know that organization

would loss from its television competitions, even it would dismiss who if KBTZ television station

should not choose to change at this moment, such as the negative outcomes would be made and

KBTZ 's managers and associates would suffer if changes were not made. Moreover, this business

manager also needed to remind every department members that as well as who also needed to downward

members to know this who individual would need to change to adopt this new organization change

culture to every department in large meetings. Even, this new director also needed to let every

department manager (leader) to know how this change process needed to carry on and every

department manager also needed to implement evaluation systems to track every department's

group individual expected behaviours and work performance whether whose work were more

efficiently or whose work were not more efficiently during this KBTZ organization was carrying

on changing at the same time. Hence, every department manager could create efficient reward

systems that reinforce every department's group individual's expected behaviours and who could

also ensure that whether the hiring and promotion systems which could support all departments colleagues new demands. Especially, news departments felt low reward dissatisfaction. Hence,

it could measure whether who ought to raise reward or who ought not to raise reward

of their work performance to evaluate more efficiently and effectively.

In conclusion, this KBTZ organization leader (new director) ought attempt to let all departments

staffs to know why it needed to change organization style and what would be the disadvantages to any

departments colleagues if it decided not change at this moment. Then, I believed that department

staffs complaints would be reduced and who would feel more fair to pay reward after who knew

how who needed to do whose task to adopt this employer to feel satisfactory.

CHAPTER III

learning how facility management influences organizational behavior

The relationship between FM and organizational behavior

The facility management has evolved as rapidly developing sector since last few decades. Facilities management has a central role to support business and must be strongly tied with the organisation's strategy in general. Facilities management has developed in the past decade into a major, flourishing business sector and discipline and continues to develop in many countries. The term facilities management has been acknowledged by governments, the business community, educationalists and researchers as vital constituent of business world. Facilities management has great significance to organisations. It has become the focus for the important issues of best value and customer satisfaction within the management of supporting services.

The significance of facility management is well recognized in many companies because there is necessity of properly managing complex and luxurious support facilities (Kincaid, 1994). The tasks are multi-disciplinary and encompasses array of activities, responsibilities, and knowledge. If services are properly managed, it enables an organisation to function in efficient and effective way, provide real added value improvements to core business. Facilities management is being promoted to a strategic level of importance and is therefore being given the task and opportunity to contribute to business success and to help the delivery of competitive advantage. Currently, the range of services covered within the responsibility of facilities management and it makes complex to the process. Facilities management has moved into the core operational functions of client organisations. It is required for facilities management service providers and their customers to recognize the role of facilities management in the organisation's strategic operations.

Concept of facility management: The notion of Facility Management was evolved in the United States in the 1970s in the business sector of outsourced services. The purpose was to respond to companies‘ demand to have a capable and specialized single-handed point of reference able to optimise all the activities concerning the management of supplementary internal services which support the business organization. Facility Management has developed with the plan of integrating and coordinating more than one service and accomplishing cost-efficiency for the client. Facilities management is described as an integrated approach to operating, maintaining, improving and adapting the buildings and infrastructure of an organisation in order to create an environment that strongly supports the primary objectives of that organisation' (Barrett and Baldry, 2003). It is also explained as 'the practice of coordinating the physical workplace with the people and work of the organisation. It integrates the principles of business administration, architecture and the behavioural and engineering sciences‘. According to Curcio (2003), Facility Management is the integrated management of all no-core business services (for buildings, space and persons) in order to run and maintain the real estate. Theoretical studies have demonstrated that Facilities management is the incorporation of processes within an organisation to maintain and develop the agreed services which support and improve the efficacy of its primary activities.

The IFMA model of a triangle of 'Ps‘, explains facility management in today's work environment that consists of people, process and place. These three factors are mutually dependent and have direct reciprocal relationships. As Armstrong (1982) designated that "we know there is a need to manage the physical environment in concert with people and job processes." Facilities management finds management solutions by positioning itself at the connection of these three factors.

Triangle of 'Ps' and FM (Source: IFMA). Facility Management

Facilities management covers multi-disciplinary activities within the built environment and the management of their impact upon people and the place of work. Successful facility management leads to work places which better support the flow of productive processes while adding value and decreasing costs. The scope, range of services, activities, responsibilities, skills and knowledge of facility management are all intended to better incorporate existing organisational factors.

Kincaid elucidated facilities management as a support role or service, part of the organisation's non-core business (supply side), and serving the requirements of major activities or core business (demand side). The function of FM is to reunite, through time, these demand and supply aspects in the organization. According to IFMA model, facilities management works in the area of place, but with obligations to support the needs of the people and processes associated with those places.

What is Facility Management? Who manages one of your organization's largest assets with one of the largest operating budgets? Facility management (FM) is a profession that encompasses multiple disciplines to ensure functionality, comfort, safety and efficiency of the built environment by integrating people, place, process and technology. Facility managers (FMs) can have many different titles and arrive in their profession through a variety of career paths. They're responsible for making sure systems of the built environment, or facility, work harmoniously. They are important because they make sure the places in which people work, play, learn and live are safe, comfortable, productive and sustainable.People Technology Graphics

FMs contribute to the organization's bottom line through their responsibility for maintaining what are often an organization's largest and most valuable assets, such as property, buildings, equipment and other environments that house personnel, productivity, inventory and other elements of operation. Here are some of the ways FMs contribute to an organization's business strategy and bottom line:

Impacting operational efficiencies
Supporting productivity of facilities and personnel
Managing risks to facilities and personnel
Mitigating environmental impact
Promoting sustainable tactics for long-term cost management
Leveraging technological solutions
Reducing or overcoming effects of natural disasters
Guaranteeing compliance
Leveraging security

Facilities management encompasses a range of disciplines and services to ensure the functionality, comfort, safety and efficiency of a built environment — buildings and grounds, infrastructure and real estate.

It includes:

Operations and maintenance
Communications management
Emergency management and business continuity
Environmental stewardship and sustainability
Hospitality
Human factors and ergonomics
Project management
Real estate and property management[2]

As a facilities manager it is likely that you will be responsible for the financial management of the services you manage. Whether it be budgeting, forecasting, or reconciliation, to be successful you need to be confident that you are managing the monetary aspects of your services. For more information, you might consider an FMP accreditation since within the syllabus Finance and Business is covered. Financial management in any business is key to success. In facilities management, not allowing the budget to run away with itself, planning and reviewing spending is important. There are many ways to keep tight financial control; these are our top 8 tips.

Facility management, or FM, is a broad discipline that includes a variety of industries, from food to technology, manufacturing to e-commerce and beyond. But, though the core of each business may be completely different from even its closest competition, successful facility management practices are easily interchangeable from enterprise to enterprise. As a matter of fact, it is one of the only job titles that can be found in, basically, any small to large organizations, including public entities, like schools and hospitals, to private businesses, like those that manage their inventory in warehouses.

Facility Management

But, reciprocal tendencies aside, facility management procedures and techniques must be highly-specialized for the business in which they are being used. Because the discipline covers complex specifics, including business continuity planning and even fire safety, it's key that your organization offers a holistic outlook on its facility management procedures.

According to the International Facilities Management Association (IFMA), facility management is an interdisciplinary practice that "considers the coordination of people, place, process, and technology." Broken down, this means that a facility manager is responsible for the success of the all facets of the facility, including organization, safety, security, and maintenance, along with the key, everyday operational practices. Facility Management Core Competencies

It may seem like an overwhelming job to put on one person or one small team – and it is an overwhelming job – but what's important to remember is the fact that facility management is just one aspect of what makes a healthy business. Simply put, all necessary departments must work with facility managers to build a business' overall success.

Here's what the discipline of facility management encompasses – and why poor management could easily lead to an organization's demise:

Safety – It's the facility management team's job to ensure the safety of all of the employees and customers occupying the property. This responsibility spans all possible environmental health and safety issues, particularly ones that concern the building and its equipment, specifically. Failure to do so can mean serious business in the form of fines, lost business, or even prosecution if it was deemed that the manager or business' negligence caused casualties or permanent environmental damage. Fire, for example, is usually right at the top of the radars of facility managers because it's a preventable tragedy that, when prepared for sufficiently, can save lives and valuable inventory. A thorough facility management team can protect its company best by guaranteeing that all parts of the facility are up-to-code, its employees are trained well, and all permits and certificates are completely valid. This function entails everything from safe and efficient lighting to flooring choices.

Security – In regards to importance, second to safety is facility security, yet another important piece of the puzzle in which the facility management team must answer to. Though larger companies or ones with particularly pricey inventory or equipment might make the wise choice to outsource its security needs in the form of a private firm, it's still the role of the facility manager to ensure that the firm performs competently. Technology advancements like biometrics and wearables are making it possible to maintain strict access control for high-security areas, but it's up to facility managers to stay on top of these developments and make smart security technology investments. In addition to general safety, it's also important that the facility management team has the technological know-how to safeguard and maintain its priciest hardware. This role is a key one as it doubly affirms that assets are protected just as closely as the safety of the community.

Maintenance and Inspections – No matter the focus of the organization, one of the most heedless things that a facility management team can do is slack off on its building maintenance duties. Every part of the building, including installed machinery such as HVAC systems, must be maintained by the facility management team. Because some facilities contain countless elements that need regular maintenance, establishing and following strict maintenance schedules helps to ensure that all moving and permanent parts of the facility stay up-to-date and working well into the future. Along with general maintenance, inspections are also something that facility management teams must always be ready for. They can prepare the business by conducting internal inspections, as needed, for the many formal regulatory inspections they might incur annually. Of course, the team must also take into account any time the facility undergoes a major change in hardware, level of inventory, or capacity – and, they must also keep their eyes on all changes in laws that could affect their current procedures.

Business Continuity Planning – Part of leading an effective facility management team means planning for "worst case scenarios." This means that each team must sit down with the powers that be to come up with a plan in case disaster strikes and the business can't afford to shut down operations. For example, let's say that a community college endures a major fire and the authorities have deemed the entire main building a total loss. The community college is currently in the middle of a semester which it can't cut short – this is a situation where prior business continuity planning is key. If this were done in the aforementioned scenario, the facility management team would have already come up with alternate locations to hold classes and operate the organization's administrative duties. In addition to the new venue, the team would have already made a solid plan for the temporary facility's security, maintenance, and hardware needs.

Daily Operational Duties – In addition to serving as the safety and security liaisons for the facility, it's also important that facility management teams are organized to handle the inherent day-to-day challenges that might arise. Depending on how the given organization is structured, this can mean anything from mending a leaky roof in the women's restroom to even fixing a jammed fax machine.

Maintenance Operations

No matter the size of the organization, it's key that the higher-ups bring on a facility manager that can hire or outsource a reliable, competent team. And, because not every company is filled with safety-minded individuals, it is the job of this manager to act as an advocate for the workers and/or customers that occupy their facility. Having this level of tenacity and attention-to-detail in the facility management spectrum is necessary – in fact, it can save a business or even a life.

Operations and Management Strategies

The current presiding global facilities management organization, the International Facility Management Association, calls for these leaders to take a more tactical and shrewd approach when it comes to protecting the future of their business' properties.

In the IFMA's Strategic Facility Planning white paper, the organization makes a call for facility managers to carry out SFP (strategic facility planning) as it "helps to avoid mistakes, delays, disappointments, and customer dissatisfaction." In addition to the aforementioned safety and maintenance-heavy responsibilities, the IFMA wants managers to begin looking beyond their normal duties so that they can better aid in the efficiency of their organizations.

To do this effectively, managers must compile two things: 1) a strategic facility plan and 2) a master plan for the facility. Let's take a look at how each one can better strengthen the overall productivity of the business:

Strategic Facility Plan (SFP) – In order to compile a comprehensive SFP, the IFMA urges managers to first become acquainted with three very important things: the core values or changing values of the organization and how facilities must reflect the values, the compiling of an in-depth analysis of the facility, including location, capability, and condition, and, finally, a fundamental understanding of how the organization's goals might make for the ramping up or down in regards to facilities. If the manager can confirm each and every one of these benchmarks with the appropriate departments and find a way to support their organization's ambitions while carrying out effective day-to-day practices, then they will be acting as a truly "strategic" support system. This blend of "current" and "future" allows for all parties involved to grapple with changes as they come in the most effective manner possible.

Facility Master Plan – Any facility manager should already be constantly re-working their facility's master plan, a framework that looks at the "physical environments that incorporate the buildings," but that doesn't mean that each is as comprehensive as it could be. Let's take a look at what a holistic master plan that takes both the day-to-day tasks as well as the future space use analyses into consideration.

Because the name of the game for facility managers is safety, maintenance, and planning, it surely comes as no surprise to you that the manager must also develop and execute a laundry list of projects to ensure that everything on and in the building is running smoothly. Facility Management Equipment Log

Here are some examples of how project management tactics can streamline a facility's overall efficiency:

Demand Organization

Of course, addressing all issues of infrastructure first is paramount to ensuring the safety and security of the facility.

Best Leadership Practices for Facility Managers

As you've already surmised, facility management is a big, often complex job that requires a strong, forward-thinking, and most of all, responsible leader who thinks about their facility's needs in as holistic of a manner as possible. In addition to possessing these qualities, the most informed managers either have years of diverse industry experience under the belt or have earned a specialized degree in the discipline. Continuing education is also common in the field, and there are a number of facilities management courses that can help facility managers stay up-to-date on current trends and best practices.

Facility Management Role

So, now that we have an idea of what an adept facility manager might look like on paper, let's delve into the most effective leadership practices they can implement to guarantee the safety and efficiency of their organization:

They are on the same page as the higher-ups in regards to the future – As mentioned throughout this guide, being a powerful facility manager means looking ahead into the future. From compiling business continuity plans in the event of a disaster to keeping an open line of communication with other departments, the manager understands that they will only be a true leader if their facility and staff are ready to roll with the changes.

They know how to plan and budget – Facility managers know the current value of every part of their facility's infrastructure – and how much it will take to upgrade. They also have an acute understanding of how their budgetary needs might ebb and flow moving forward so that they can accurately propose budgetary changes to the powers that be.

They have a feel for developing a great team – Depending on the specific needs of the organization, the facility manager might be responsible for the hiring and training of the facility workers, contractors, or even consultants. This means that the manager needs to have an innate understanding of the duties and restraints of each position and how they can best work together to make the most capable team possible. Remember, these team members are ultimately in control of the safety and security of the facility, very important jobs that can break an organization in regards to liability if something were to go awry.

They are willing to listen – It's only natural for facility managers to become frustrated with higher-ups calling for big shifts who might be physically disconnected with the facility, but that doesn't mean that they are wrong. Dynamic leaders collaborate with all departments by listening to their propositions and ideas. By doing so, they create an open, safe line of communication that, no matter the outcome, will strengthen interdepartmental relations.

Facility management is a challenging job, and it's one that grows increasingly complex as technology advancements reshape old processes into newer, streamlined approaches. The best facility managers understand exactly how to balance smart technology investments that boost efficiency while minimizing risks (e.g., fiscal and safety risks) for a positive influence on the bottom line. In short, facility management is the backbone of operations across a multitude of industries today.

Failities Management Budget Planning

One of the most difficult tasks for any facilities manager is budget planning and management. Trying to account for workplace expenses can seem like an insurmountable job. Nevertheless, it's one you'll have to face head-on. Here are a few tips to conquer budget issues:

1. Look at costs

Understanding how to budget for facility management starts with understanding the various costs of running your workplace. Everything from maintenance costs to expenses for routine maintenance throughout affect how much you spend above and beyond your lease.

Fixed and known costs

Start by tabulating your fixed costs. For example, if you know you pay $12,000 per year for landscaping, you can budget this as a fixed cost. Likewise, if you have access to pricing from vendors and partners for products and services to be purchased in the year ahead, budget those as known costs.

Unknown and unexpected costs

What's harder to plan for are unforeseen costs. There are a few ways to make the unexpected more predictable. Use historical data for things like routine maintenance costs. Depending on the quality of your records, you can also look at costs from years past and match those to expenditures you may face.

One-off and seasonal costs

It's a good idea to break down costs on a monthly, quarterly, and annual basis. This will help highlight overlooked costs, such as seasonal facility fees. For example, you may pay more for utilities in the winter and more for landscaping in the summer. Similarly, if you want to plan a renovation in the spring, you'll be able to more easily account for those costs when your budget is broken down.

2. Look at trends

You may not have a crystal ball for telling the future, but if you're up on workplace trends, it could be the next best thing. One of the best budgeting tips for facilities managers is looking closely at workplace and facility management trends and budgeting for them.

Will you be making any changes to your physical workplace layout this year? If so, you'll need to budget for each part of the project. Expanding your office IoT this year? Accounting for the integration costs should be the focal point.

Everything outside the normal scope of day-to-day facilities management will come at a cost. The key to building an inclusive budget is planning.

3. Look at the little things

Your facility management budget is complex, but that doesn't mean it should be convoluted. Just like integrated facilities management is a rising trend, integrated budgeting is also important. This means budgeting for your facilities through different lenses.

Take your facilities management budget and break it into individual segments. Look at costs for running each part of your facility, then build a strategy to make the most of those dollars. For example, buying lightbulbs may seem simple. But is that ongoing cost more than researching a more-efficient lighting solution? Forcing yourself to budget at scale also forces you to think about the cumulative elements of your workplace.

4. Build in a buffer

Even the best budget is one unforeseen cost away from being busted. That is, of course, you build in a buffer.

First, take the sub-budgets that comprise your overall facilities budget and build in dollars for miscellaneous expenses. This will give you some wiggle room at a more subtle level. For example, if you're under budget in one area and over budget in another, a simple transfer can balance things out.

Alternatively, you can pad the top of your budget with one lump sum for general, unexpected expenses. This tactic provides a lump sum to work with later on.

5. Sell it to the C-suite

Perhaps the hardest part of budgeting for facilities management is selling it to executives. Illustrate value wherever possible and justify expenses with benefits. If you've taken the time to budget well and responsibly account for contingencies, you won't have to defend your budget so much as explain it. Draw connections from your budget to the impact they have on the workplace and stand by your costs and figures.

Budgeting is never easy, no matter what line of work you're in. For facilities managers, there's a lot to consider and a lot that's unknown. The more you account for your variables, recognize trends, and build in a buffer, the more comfortable you'll feel in your final budget. Note: make sure to double-check numbers.

According to Reliability Web, maintenance management typically makes up 40% to 50% of operational budgets. Therefore, the possible savings from increased efficiency, such as the ability to spend money where it will create the most value and reducing the number of unnecessary maintenance orders, is significant. Supporting this, Transcendent reported that the average company can save between 12% and 18% of their maintenance budgets by prioritizing preventive maintenance over reactive maintenance.

Understanding historical facility data can empower stakeholders to create a best-in-class facility management budget. Likewise, the careful consideration of reactive and preventive maintenance needs, as well as of plans for spending capital on replacement equipment, can benefit budget creation. As will be reviewed below, by using strategic resource planning, emphasizing preventive maintenance and thoughtfully deploying a capitalization policy, facility managers can successfully forecast costs. This includes taking steps such as:

Creating a framework for maintenance expenses

Considering capital projects

Aligning labor and inventory availability

Leaving some wiggle room

Working with a facility management partner

A firm foundation of insights informed by data can be leveraged for accurate capital planning.

Accurate data unlocks the potential of facility budgets

Armed with historical facility data, industry trends and capital project plans, facility managers can determine which percentage of their budgets to allocate to reactive maintenance, preventative measures and capital investments. However, facility managers who work with distributed locations often struggle to make sense of large volumes of data, which can make it difficult to establish budget parameters.

A facility management partner such as Vixxo can fill in this gap by leveraging more than 45 million industry- and region-specific data to inform pricing. Work order data includes:

Labor rates

Material costs

Average work order duration

Trip charges

Regional taxes

It's important to have this information since each type of data impacts budgetary spending. For example, knowing material costs ahead of time can help stakeholders to determine if they are overspending on work orders.

Additionally, a management partner such as Vixxo can implement an asset tagging program to accurately track, monitor, and analyze equipment performance. Access to this granular data allows facility stakeholders to forecast their future resource needs, which is important knowledge to possess when budget allocations shift over time.

For instance, 45% of facility managers saw their operating budgets increase between 2016 and 2017, as reported by FacilitiesNet. Similarly, 40% saw their capital budgets increase over the same period. In other words, facility managers may have more money to allocate than in previous years. Historical facility and industry data will help managers determine where this investment can best contribute to organizational growth. For example, access to additional resources may allow stakeholders to work on projects that were previously delayed due to lack of resources.

To determine how best to forecast facilities spend, stakeholders need access to actionable data. In fact, best-in-class companies are 74% more likely than their peers to provide easy access to facility data for employees. However, this data is just one piece of a larger puzzle.

Key tips for forecasting facility management costs

While there's no one-size-fits-all solution that suits facilities of all types, there is a strategy that can support creating a budget: Determining short- and long-term expenditures, forecasting vendor costs and developing a plan for unexpected expenses. Enterprises with distributed locations may also need to develop unique budgets for each region.

Tip #1: Create a framework for maintenance expenses

Pain point: How can you account for all expenses that should be considered in a maintenance budget?

Solution: Factor in historical and industry data to best forecast future needs.

According to The National Academies of Sciences, Engineering and Medicine, an appropriate budget allocation for routine maintenance and repair for most facilities typically ranges from 2% to 4% of the aggregate current replacement value of the facility, excluding land and major infrastructure.

For example, if the aggregate replacement value of all equipment within a facility is $1 million, then a safe minimum maintenance budget would be between $20,000 and $40,000.

Vendor costs should not be ignored. The ability to accurately forecast spend is easier when you prioritize preventive actions because there will be fewer unexpected equipment failures, but no one can predict the future for certain. Historical facility and industry data can provide some guidance. Likewise, allocating additional resources for preventive maintenance can reduce repair and replacement costs down the line.

Actively used equipment isn't all that needs to be monitored. The budget should address the preventive maintenance needs of exterior structures such as parking lots, roofs and building facades. When these major assets are not routinely maintained, it accelerates their deterioration and increases long-term spend.

An effective maintenance budget framework utilizes industry best practices informed by tailored data and historical facility trends.

Tip #2: Consider capital projects

Pain point: How can you ensure that capital projects don't consume resources intended for maintenance?

Solution: Establish a capitalization policy that creates spending thresholds.

Beyond routine maintenance and repair, the budget should reflect upcoming construction projects. According to IndustryWeek, approximately 33% of capital projects under $500 million are late or over budget. The budget allotment for construction will vary greatly depending on the extent of the project, impact on human resources and regulatory concerns. A capitalization policy reduces record-keeping costs and ensures projects don't exceed budget allocations.

A capitalization policy is used to set a threshold. Expenditures above the threshold are recorded as fixed assets - any asset with a useful life beyond a single reporting period - and expenditures below the threshold are charged as incurred expenses. Best-in-class enterprises will use a programmatic approach utilizing facility maintenance data to make decisions pertaining to capital.

Facility managers know how to create effective maintenance budgets. After all, who knows your facility better than you? Your facilities expertise, combined with the knowledge of a facility management partner, can help you save money by monitoring your facility and equipment performance, identifying trends and uncovering opportunities.

Connect with an expert consultant at Vixxo to learn more about how to align industry best practices with your organization's unique pain points. A conversation can help you understand how a standardized budgeting method is essential in creating optimized operational budgets. Vixxo's wide range of solutions provide holistic visibility into every transaction at the equipment level and gives you the strategic intelligence you need to grow your business.

Five steps in navigating the facilities management outsourcing journey

Are your campus facilities operations aligned with your mission?

Facing growing competition for students and limited resources to address facilities issues, many public and private institutions are seeking creative new facility management approaches. If you're considering options for improving your facility management operating model, you may be evaluating the benefits of facility management outsourcing.

Aligning your mission and your campus real estate operations doesn't happen by accident—it's the result of stakeholder collaboration and thoughtful consideration of your goals and possible solutions. When carefully crafted, a facility management partnership can be a strategic solution for reining in costs, improving quality of service and enhancing the campus experience for students, faculty staff and alumni alike. How you navigate your way through the outsourcing decision and the launch of your facility management partnership will make all the difference in ensuring that your goals are achieved.

Facility management has the potential to deliver cost savings, reduce energy consumption, improve sustainability and— most important—enhance the quality of your facilities and the campus experience.

Executed properly, outsourcing facility management can help you attract and retain talented students, faculty and staff. Through highly visible campus improvements and smooth running real estate operations, outsourced facility management can deliver long-term cost savings by addressing deferred maintenance energy consumption and sustainability. Most importantly, it can enhance the quality of your facilities and the campus experience overall.

Yet, closing the gap between the potential of outsourced facility management and its ideal outcomes can be a challenge. Despite the benefits it can deliver, the topic of facility management outsourcing may spark concerns about job loss, service disruption and a decline in campus quality. You can overcome the misperceptions and help close the gap—if you undertake the outsourcing journey with thoughtful planning.

Outsourcing can advance your facility management goals through access to innovative ideas, leading practices and new facility management technologies. And, it eases the headaches of managing the physical campus.

Take a look at your facility management infrastructure. Are you using leading technologies to improve building efficiency, save energy and streamline facility management functions? Do your building engineers use predictive and preventative maintenance strategies to keep building systems running smoothly? Do your systems track data space utilization data so you can optimize usage and avoid the cost of new construction?

Wireless sensors, automation, machine learning and artificial intelligence are bringing new efficiency and data-driven decision making to facility management. However, many higher education institutions have yet to capitalize on facility management advances that are commonplace among leading facility management service provider firms.

Do you have a process for prioritizing capital investments? Have you created a capital plan that balances repairs, replacements and modernization? Following the construction boom of the past decade, many colleges and universities now are revisiting campus upkeep. A facility management partner can assess your campus facilities, establish priorities and help you create a five-year campus plan.

Have you implemented a comprehensive energy and sustainability program? Leading practices include more than 50 ways to reduce your institution's carbon footprint, from simple waste-reduction measures to adopting alternative energy sources.

Are you capitalizing on opportunities for strategic sourcing and volume discounts on vendor services? A leading facility management service provider can deliver savings through its wholesale supplier agreements, reducing procurement expenses.

Aligning facility management with your institutional mission can be easier when you have a seasoned partner to offer data-driven recommendations and expertise based on their experience. However, defining your outsourcing path requires careful thought and consideration.

Partnering with a facility management service provider isn't an all-ornothing proposition. It's critical to consider the best ways to advance your facility management practices to better support your mission. Drawing from our work with public and private colleges and universities, we've identified the following key steps that can help ensure a successful partnering journey.

Top facility management service providers typically can reduce your long-term operating expenses by anywhere from five to 30 percent through operational efficiencies

1. Clarify your facility goals.

Without clear expectations, a partnership can easily get off track. First, consider what sparked your interest in outsourcing. What do you hope to achieve? You may simply wish to spend less time and energy on facilities issues and more on core educational mission concerns. You may be concerned about deferred maintenance and facilities costs, or seeking creative new approaches to improve efficiency.

Integrated facility management outsourcing can be a powerful tool. While you're focused on your mission, your facility management partner will hire and train your knowledgeable associates in the latest campus real estate technologies and optimize use of your integrated workplace management system. They'll help you adopt a data driven approach to managing your campus. They'll apply leading practices to keep your building operations running smoothly. They'll bring innovative new approaches to the challenges of your real estate.

Following the initial expense of the outsourcing transition, your service provider will help you reduce costs over time. By tackling deferred maintenance, prioritizing investments, self-performing equipment repairs and adopting preventative maintenance strategies, an experienced facility management service provider will bring new efficiency and performance to your campus.

Aside from day-to-day tactical needs, consider the larger picture. Rather than simply out-tasking functions such as groundskeeping or custodial services, some colleges and universities have achieved more cost savings and more productive campuses by centralizing the entire facility management function under an integrated full-service provider.

In energy management, workflow management, supply chain management and workforce administration. Not only do you reduce your facility management headaches, but the cost savings also translate directly into better stewardship of university resources, a more attractive campus, and more engaged students, faculty and staff.

In a properly developed, full-service, integrated facility management partnership, an experienced partner will be as committed to your educational mission as you are, and will establish shared goals with you. Only when both parties are fully invested in the relationship, as true partners, can you achieve your ideal outcomes.

2. Collaborate with internal campus stakeholders to identify your facilities management needs and issues.

Collaborating with key stakeholders in a discussion of your campus needs and goals is an important step toward better alignment of facilities operations with your mission. When you want to bring innovation, leading practices and data-driven decision making to your real estate operations, stakeholder conversations will help clarify how facility management outsourcing could be part of the solution, and build consensus for your desired outcomes. Stakeholders may include your CFO, COO, board of trustees or directors, director of facilities, senior leaders for academics, enrollment and retention, human resources, housing, athletics, etc. Each will have a unique set of needs and concerns.

Before broaching these topics with your stakeholders, however, it's wise to meet informally with potential facility management service providers. A leading provider will provide you with valuable insights about how facility management outsourcing could help achieve your campus vision. And, the firm's executives will address your questions and address any misperceptions you may have about what to expect. These preliminary conversations will lead to more productive conversations with your stakeholders because you'll be better prepared to address their concerns.

For example, department heads may be focused on quality of service and ensuring that their faculty and students have modern, well-maintained spaces that advance research and learning. Enrollment and retention executives, on the other hand, may focus on "curb appeal" and amenities that will help attract students.

Once your senior leadership has reached consensus on pursuing facility management outsourcing, you'll need to engage your facilities staff. First and foremost, they'll naturally have questions about their jobs and roles that you'll need to address clearly. Second, they can provide valuable information about critical issues they see on campus.

These early conversations are a critical opportunity to address misperceptions and concerns about outsourcing. Facilities associates will naturally be concerned about job loss—staff reduction is a common misconception about outsourcing.

The reality is that a reputable partner will be eager to hire your facilities associates and retain their valuable institutional knowledge. In fact, facility management associates who transition to your facility management service provider firm will likely discover new career advancement and learning opportunities.

Upfront collaboration will uncover your campus facility management priorities. And, upfront engagement with stakeholders will help create buy-in for whatever solutions you pursue.

3. Explore options for achieving the desired outcomes.

With stakeholder perspectives in mind, you're ready to explore the best ways to achieve the outcomes you've envisioned. You may be able to achieve some of these with adjustments to your current operating model. For others, partnering with a facility management service provider may be the best way to access new approaches.

Often, a college or university will initially outsource custodial, groundskeeping services or energy and sustainability, but this out-tasking is only one part of possible solution. The leading facility management service providers offer numerous options for accessing facilities services at various levels.

To access cutting-edge facility management technologies, for instance, you could license a mobile end-to-end work-order management application that generates valuable business intelligence and audit trails. To tackle deferred maintenance, you could retain a building assessment and asset management service for data-driven capital planning and maintenance. Or, you could partner with a facility management firm to provide variable building engineering services to augment your in-house team.

4. Design a transparent contract aligned with your interests and desired facilities outcomes.

Given the complexity and importance of facilities management, the traditional procurement process does not always deliver a successful partnership. Traditional procurement often begins with a request for proposal (RFP) that specifies exactly how the work will be performed, rather than asking the service provider to propose creative solutions to achieve certain goals. And, traditional contracts usually lack meaningful mechanisms for measuring performance and rewarding performance that exceeds target outcomes.

In contrast, the maturation of outsourced facility management has led to the adoption of outcomes-based 'vested' contracts that focus on agreed-upon outcomes and key performance indicators rather than on predefined tasks. In performance-based contracts, the partner's fees typically are reduced if goals aren't met, while shared savings and bonuses are provided for exceeding targets. Incorporating fees-at-risk, vested outsourcing creates a transparent, win-win relationship that achieves outcomes rather than predefined tasks.

It is critically important to explore procurement options for facility management services. Challenge your procurement team to provide options and to collaborate with reputable facility management companies to identify alternatives to traditional procurement methods. The final contract should be aligned with your desired outcomes, while allowing the facility management provider flexibility to deliver services using its own expertise. The partner can determine the most cost-effective, sustainable approach.

Ideally, your partnership will give your service provider the flexibility to customize their work with you, with financial incentives to meet or exceed the goals that you jointly define. And, your contract should address governance—how the partnership will be managed and by whom. Your partnership is much more likely to achieve its goals if you first establish, in plain language, how you will manage the contractual relationship. Through these measures, the service provider's work will be closely aligned with supporting your mission—and you will open the door to bringing leading practices and innovative new approaches to your facilities operations.

5. Communicate clearly—and often—to manage a smooth transition.

Whether you outsource some facility management functions or choose a full-service partnership, managing the change will require thoughtful communications before, during and afterwards to prevent negative misperceptions from undermining the overall experience.

Facility management associates will naturally have questions about their jobs and the prospect of transitioning to a service provider. It's critical to convey that a leading facility management service provider will want to hire your knowledgeable associates to continue supporting your facilities.

Administrators, faculty and students, meanwhile, will likely want assurance that the facilities staff they know and trust will still be on hand. They may have concerns about levels of service or accessing services. They will want to know that the service provider, once selected, is reputable and committed to honouring both the institution's mission and the transitioning employees.

Once selected, your service provider should collaborate with you to create and implement a thoughtful communications plan that anticipates and addresses important issues. The plan should include consistent messages for key stakeholders and the campus community as a whole, and provide opportunities for facility management professionals to discuss their concerns in one-on-one meetings with your facilities leadership.

Also critical, allow time for a smooth transition. Typically, the service provider will need 90 days to onboard transitioning employees, depending on the scope of the partnership. During the transition period, your facility management partner will ensure that transitioned associates are informed about their pay and benefits, and equipped to apply their new employer's technologies and processes to benefit your campus. Also important, transitioned associates can begin to consider their professional development opportunities.

We did not find results for: What is Strategic Facility Planning (SFP) and 4 steps to conquer itThe type, quantity and location are important to the SFP process, which encompasses understanding, analysing, planning and acting for the long term.In order for FM providers to effectively address the needs of public sector organizations, it is imperative to move beyond Facility Management and engage in a degree of Strategic Facility Planning (SFP). SFP identifies the type, quantity and location of spaces required to fully support the organizations business initiatives and should be framed within the organization's vision.SFP includes three primary components An understanding of the organization's culture and core values and an analysis of how existing and new facilities must manifest that culture and core values within the physical space or support their change; an in-depth analysis of existing facilities – including location, capability, utilization and condition; and an achievable and affordable plan that translates the goals of the business plan into an appropriate facility response.SFP described as a four-step process1. Understanding: The thorough understanding the organisation's mission, vision, values, and goals;2. Analysing: The analysis of the organization's facility needs;3. Planning: The development of strategies that meet long-term needs of the organization;4. Acting: The implementation of planned strategies.As SFP merges with strategic policy objectives of each particular sector.

Facility Planning: Steps, Process, Objectives, Importance

Facility PlanningFacility planning or strategic facility planning recognizes that every decision made in business planning has a direct impact on an organization's real estate assets and needs.

In the real world of facility management, a plethora of activities falls under the facility manager's responsibility, causing frequent lapses into a reactive mode to respond to all the requests, orders, regulations, deadlines and demands of the organization.

Facilities are the critical components of an organization's strategic facility planning since they are the outcome of business decision-making processes and have a long-term impact on the support for the achievement of the organization's mission and vision.

Linking facilities to core business strategies is one of the imperatives of refined facility management now and in the future. Even greater importance will be given to strategic facility planning in the coming years as budgets continue to be squeezed and worker performance and productivity are key factors in the knowledge age.

strategic facility planning facilitates the organization's strategy by optimizing facilities to satisfy the strategic relationships between the organization, products/services, and facilities.

The strategic facility planning is a two-to-five year plan encompassing the entire portfolio of owned and/or leased space that sets strategic facility goals based on the organization's strategic objectives.

Strategic facility planning helps facility managers do a better job and ensures that all employees are working toward the same goals and objectives.

4 Steps of Facility Planning

A flexible and implementable strategic facility planning based on the specific and unique considerations of your organization needs to be developed through a 4 step process.

4 step process of understanding the situation, facilities, conditions, and expectations, analyzing the needs and changes required, planning, and then executing an approved plan will be explained.

Numerous tools for each step of the four-step process will also be suggested.

4 steps of strategic facility planning process

4 step process of facility planning are;

Understanding.

Analyzing.

Planning.

Acting.

1. Understanding

The first step, understanding, requires a thorough knowledge of your organization's mission, vision, values, and goals.

Thoroughly understand the organization's mission, vision, values, and goals.

Many organizations follow a balanced scorecard of 4 key measurements: financial performance; customer knowledge; internal business processes; and learning and growth.

The strategic plan focuses on the longer-term, big-picture needs and vision of the organization. Because the SFP meshes with the strategic business plan of each unique organization, alignment is critical for success.

Facility managers must begin the development of the SFP by thoroughly understanding the needs of the organization.

Through existing internal analysis and business imperatives, the work that an SFP team completes is entirely dependent upon the organization's specific needs and should address both strategic and long-range planning.

Conversely, it should also address the evaluation of current facilities and the conceptualization, planning, and implementation of new facilities.

A thorough understanding of the current situation is necessary to properly analyze the needs
and compare existing conditions to those needs.

Commonly, strategic plans provide a combination and range of recommendations to maximize the value of a corporation's assets.

The facility manager considers factors such as: the organization's mission, vision, culture and core values; the current position of the business and its current real estate asset base; its overall direction and the projects currently underway within the corporation; how the business may change; and how those changes may affect the real estate needs of the corporation.

Once these considerations are well understood, a business-driven approach is taken to analyze the organization's facilities and to set tangible goals and plan targets.

Often, organizations take a strictly cost-driven approach to their facilities.

Although they are quick to implement and are often cost-effective, this approach is nevertheless lacking in vision, fails to adequately address the actual delivery of the business goods and/or services, and has only a moderate long-term impact on improving the overall performance of the business as a whole.

In contrast, a business-driven approach despite necessitating a longer timeframe delivers a clear vision for the future, earns employee support and enhances performance, which strengthens the business competitively.

Using this business-driven approach, the team studies the real estate assets that the corporation currently holds using gathered data, modeling tools, and scenario alternatives.

This data often includes lease and ownership data, building assessments, square footages, space utilization standards, and location characteristics.

To provide a comprehensive plan, the facility manager and SFP team explore the various business goals of each unit in the business and integrate these goals into the facility plan analyses.

This input defines future space and real estate needs based on overall corporate goals starting with anticipated services, expected staffing changes and potential new technologies.

The team uses these needs to predict future headcounts, demographics, space utilization, maintenance requirements, capital investment and operating costs.

At this stage, a clear understanding of the goals of the SFP, as well as the approval process and measures for success, will be complete and have the second stage follow.

2. Analyzing

Second, exploration of the range of possible futures and triggers is needed to analyze your organization's facility needs using analytical techniques — such as systematic layout planning (SLP), strengths, weaknesses, opportunities and threats analysis (SWOT), strategic creative analysis (SCAN), or scenario planning.

Use analytical techniques, such as SWOT analysis, SCAN, SLP or scenario planning, to explore the range of possible futures and the triggers used to analyze an organization's facility needs.

Once a clear definition of the business' situation has been established, the facility manager, planners, and designers begin to consider how to balance current facility needs with long-term needs and issues.

These needs and issues may include workforce demographics, manufacturing processes, organizational structure and culture, community and government regulatory requirements, market position, and capacity rates and volumes. All of these combine to define the individual elements of the SFP.

The comparison of the current inventory and conditions with the future needs provides the gap that the SP will address.

Analysis Tools

Several tools (see Analysis Tools section) may be used to compare, analyze, coordinate and clarify this gap and the alternatives, scenarios, and recommendations that are made.

Scenario Planning

Scenarios are tools for thinking ahead to anticipate the changes that will impact your organization.

Scenarios can be considered instructive simulations of possible operating conditions.

This approach might be used in conjunction with other models to ensure planners truly undertake strategic thinking.

Scenario planning may be particularly useful in identifying strategic issues and goals.

Select several external forces and imagine related changes that might influence the organization, such as the global marketplace, technology, change in regulations, demographic changes, etc. Scan newspapers and Internet sources for key headlines to suggest potential changes that may affect the organization. Utilize IFMA's and other association's trend reports.

For each potential change, discuss three different future organizational scenarios (including the best case, worst case, and all right/reasonable case), which may arise within the organization as a result of each change. Reviewing the worst-case scenario often provokes strong motivation for needed changes.

Suggest what the organization might do, or potential strategies, in each of the three scenarios to respond to each change.

Planners soon detect common considerations or strategies that must be addressed to respond to possible external changes.

Select the most likely external changes to affect the organization, over the next three to five years, for example, and identify the most reasonable strategies the organization can undertake to respond to these changes.

The product of this process is not a final, cut-in-stone document, but provides insight into how different decisions will affect the organization's return on investment, cash flow, debt load, work processes and productivity of its employees.

Scenarios will guide decision-makers and provide advance consideration of the potential impacts of different facility decisions.

Systematic Layout Planning (SLP)

The SLP method was developed by Muther (1973) to create conceptual block layouts.

The method successively adds complex data categories until a block layout has been generated, making it a strategy to the tactical tool.

Document the present operation (Deliverable: flowcharts).

Define the activities and planning horizon (Deliverable: table).

Develop activity relationships (Deliverable: relationship diagram).

Develop a square footage requirements spreadsheet (Deliverable: spreadsheet).

Develop block plan layouts (Deliverable: block plan layout).

Development of an equipment layout (Deliverable: equipment layout).

SWOT Analysis

SWOT Analysis is another planning tool used to strategically evaluate the strengths, weaknesses, opportunities, and threats in a project or a business venture.

SWOT uses business objectives and identifies both internal and external factors that are either favorable or unfavorable to achieving that objective.

The four areas considered are;

Strengths: attributes of the organization helpful to achieving the objective and describing how they can be leveraged.

Weaknesses: attributes of the organization harmful to achieving the

objective and how they can be minimized or neutralized.
Opportunities: external conditions helpful to achieving the objective.
Threats: external conditions harmful to achieving the objective.

Brainstorming (AGIR-a gang in a room)

This technique better ensures that various views and aspects are represented, particularly if the individuals are chosen well. The downside may be too much input, which may yield inconsistencies.

However, done properly, brainstorming provides an opportunity for creative, innovative concepts that might otherwise be overlooked.

As such, it is suggested that a professional facilitator should conduct these types of sessions.

Strategic Creative Analysis (SCAN)

Strategic Creative Analysis is a process for strategic planning, decision making and analyzing case studies. An example of a strategic planning technique that incorporates a SWOT analysis is SCAN analysis.

The process of SCAN is described in Exhibit 1. (Step 3. Includes the Top Rated Objective – TRO).

Benchmarking

Benchmarking is a very useful SFP tool for comparing and measuring your organization against others, anywhere in the world, to gain information on philosophies, practices, and measures that will help your organization take action to improve its performance.

In summary, benchmarking is the practice of being humble enough to admit that others are better at something and being wise enough to learn how to match, and even surpass, them at it.

Benchmarking utilizes much of the organizational understanding gained in the first step of SFP to compare practices and metrics to recognized leaders.

Networking with peer organizations, competitors, and especially for facility organizations, visiting award-winning service organizations provides insight to bring back and adapt to your operations.

Adaptation is the key—recognizing a good process or practice and use it in your specific way within your organization is the essence of successful benchmarking.

For SFP to serve as the right mechanism to analyze and improve current facility operations, a proactive approach to benchmarking practices and services of those organizations recognized as industry leaders is needed.

Benchmarking may be undertaken as part of a broader process reengineering initiative, or it might be conducted as a freestanding exercise.

Organizational Simulation

Organizational simulation is a prominent method in organizational studies and strategic management. This tool aims to understand how organizations operate.

The organizational simulation can describe the coordination of facility operations based on understanding and analyzing the impact of interrelated facility alternatives and activities.

This method can measure organizational performance and support strategic thinking.

3. Planning

Third, once the analysis is completed, plans for potential responses and periodic updates to existing plans in response to changes in the market need to be developed to meet the long-range needs of your specific organization.

Develop plans that meet the long-range needs of the organization.

At a minimum, the SFP should be reviewed annually and further updated periodically as conditions require.

As a result of the analyses performed, decisions will become apparent or recommended courses of action can be supported by the completed analysis.

These recommendations will become the essence of the SFP.

To be organizationally mandated, most facility managers will need to present the recommendations to senior management, obtain buy-in (often involving some negotiation and adjustment to the plan), and get final approval and funding for the proposed plan.

IFMA uses and recommends the balanced scorecard methodology for integrating planning into the organization's objectives, but recognizes that every organization has selected methods for business processes and facility management conforms to align with the organization's methodologies.

The following are major steps in setting up the plan:

Document the primary objectives to be addressed (the gap) in the SFP.

Evaluate sites, zoning, costs, labor, competition and all factors critical for success.

Conduct financial and risk analysis to focus on finding the maximum value.

Develop alternatives with recommendations and priorities.

Develop a process for marketing the recommended SFP to gain management approval.

Obtain financial and other approvals needed to launch the action phase.

It is important to note that once approved, the SFP may continue to evolve and adapt to changing conditions within and outside the organization. The flexibility of a good SFP will accommodate the most minor adjustments.

4. Acting / Action

Fourth, take action as planned to successfully implement the strategic facility planning.

Take actions as planned and implement the SFP. Feedback from actions taken can be incorporated into the next plan and/or project to provide continuous improvement to future SFPs.

After approval, the SFP is then ready for implementation.

Implementation of an SFP typically requires the development of a specific project or project to deliver new, altered or reconfigured space to meet the organizational need. This specific project is a unique process that is supplemental to the SFP.

Specific project planning with take place outside the SFP to fulfill the detailed implementation phase. Some projects, especially large new space projects, may be managed by specialty or contract groups.

It is critical in these cases that facilities stay involved as a core team member, to ensure integration of the planning and operational phases of the specific project.

Regardless of the tools used in the development of an SFP, the SFP should be viewed as a living document that reports findings and makes considered recommendations for implementing the plan within a realistic time frame, yet maintains flexibility to adapt as business requires.

While implementation is in progress, flexibility to adapt to changed conditions may be required.

It is prudent to view an SFP as the "current SFP" since any major change in market conditions, economic outlook or other forces could require varying degrees of change to the original document.

This is another reason that scenarios are very helpful—since they anticipate some of these potential changes. The SFP is a major facility management tool used to support the organization—alignment with the organizational vision, mission, goals, and objectives are always critical for the success of the SFP.

Documentation of especially successful or problematic portions of the SFP, if noted, can provide valuable feedback for the next iteration of planning.

The cyclical nature of planning and continuous improvement provides opportunities to learn from each process. The following diagram is a process model developed for SFP accomplishment.

This process model integrates the sequential activities, participants, deliverables and inter-relationships for an individual organization to be successful when implementing the 4-step SFP process.

The process model includes three layers of participants (executive management, facility manager and staff) and roles illustrating who implements each of the tasks in the SFP development process.

The SFP team needs to be closely connected to implement activities from the project launch through to the final implementation phase and hand-off for the development of the tactical facility plans to support the organization's business planning.

Major activities are aligned with the four-step process and include tasks such as data gathering/benchmarking, analysis/synthesis, scenario development/forecasting, and SFP implementation.

The process model ends with the hand-off to a tactical facility plan, which often is the facility management annual plan or budget.

Feedback through all phases for continuous improvement is shown with arrows in reverse. It should also be noted that there are no hard and fast lines indicating when one phase ends and the next starts.

Plans flow at different rates, due to different organizational requirements and managerial direction. The precise transitions are unimportant but need to follow your own organization's requirements.

Facility Planning and Facility Managers

Facility managers know that they need to become more proactive and strategic is important, but finding the time to devote to strategic planning is often a struggle.

As Stephen Covey teaches, we need to prioritize what is important rather than simply urgent to gain maximum effectiveness.

Strategic facility planning is a process that can lead to better, more proactive delivery of services from a facility management organization to its stakeholders.

The time taken to carry out strategic facility planning is well spent in that it helps to avoid mistakes, delays, disappointments and customer dissatisfaction.

It can allow facility plan implementations to run more quickly and smoothly.

Since strategic facility planning is not a daily task, many facility managers are unfamiliar with the best way to accomplish this type of planning, or perhaps have been asked by senior management to quickly provide a strategic facility plan and are not sure where to start.

Facility managers may still be unsure how to initiate the strategic facility planning process and need to obtain information on methods and techniques useful for successfully implementing a strategic facility planning to correspond with their organization's needs.

While every organization is different, all organizations strive to become more competitive, effective and provide the best workplace possible for its employees. This is the role facility managers fulfill and strategic facility planning is an exercise that is considered another tool to add to the "FM tool belt" needed for success.

Conclusion

The cyclical nature of constant planning for the changing future and adopting plans along the way are normal events. These changes and updates must be managed to ensure they are achievable.

The strategic facility planning identifies the type, quantity, and location of spaces needed by the organization and contains two main components the first being an in-depth analysis of existing facilities, and the other an achievable and affordable plan to meet the organization's needs.

Using the organizational business plan, the differences should be identified between the current situations and analyzed needs.

Gap analysis a business resource assessment tool enabling an organization to compare its actual performance with its potential performance is an appropriate tool to be used.

Financial analysis is also required to determine the yield on the highest return at the lowest risk.

A proactive approach to benchmark practices and services of leading organizations in the industry will be helpful for strategic facility planning and serves as a mechanism to understand, analyze and improve the current facilities operation.

Since differences in organizational type, culture and processes strongly influence how strategic facility planning is accomplished, the recommended strategic facility planning will need to be adjusted by the different types, culture, and processes of your specific organization.

The purpose of the SFP plan, therefore, is to develop a flexible and implementable plan based on the specific and unique considerations of the individual business.

Five Facilities Management Processes Every Company Needs to Implement

Facilities management processes are the backbone of a well-functioning workplace. Not only do they standardize some of the most critical workplace operations, they set the standard for how work gets done. Without defined processes, there's room for error, non-compliance, miscommunication, and mismanaged expectations—all things that stunt productivity.

The broader workplace is primed for standardization and automation. But there are several core processes to anchor first, as they set the tone for critical operations.

Here's a look at five facility management processes to implement or tighten up for a safe, productive, efficient workplace:

1. Work order submissions

What's the standard operating procedure for reporting facility issues in your workplace? If there isn't one, there needs to be. Make work order submissions and facilities requests as direct and simple as possible. Eliminating steps between problem identification and resolution is key to facilitating quick results.

For example, a submission form on your company's intranet or Slack channel for facilities issues provides employees with a direct mode of communication. It replaces "telephone tag" that can occur when an employee reports an issue to their supervisor...who then emails facilities...which contacts the facility manager...and so on.

Work order submissions are perfect for addressing employee comfort issues to fixing workplace hazards.

2. Room reservations

Lost time is a drain on productivity, resources, and revenue. Every minute employees spend trying to find the right space to work in is 60 seconds they can't get back. One of the simplest, yet most critical, facility management best practices is a room reservation system.

Reservation systems should be dynamic and adaptive, capable of handling the many moving parts of your workplace. Automate where possible. SpaceIQ's Slack integration is a great example of this. By asking Slack for a meeting room, the system automatically shows available spaces, room capacity, location, and booking options. When booked, the room appears unavailable to anyone seeking that space. It prevents the wasted minutes and frustration that come from searching for space.

Consider this: If you save 10 minutes in room searches each day, that's 43 hours a year—more than a standard work week.

3. Directory management

Your workplace should be collaborative—not just between departments, but across the entire company. In order to communicate and collaborate, employees need access to each other. This starts with an up-to-date directory.

Facility managers need a process for maintaining a real-time directory that's open and accessible. This is more of a challenge in today's dynamic workplace. Hot desks and flexible workspaces mean employees are always on the move. Remote workers have different schedules and contact information. Growing companies are constantly adding new employees.

Directory management through an Integrated Workplace Management System (read more on what is IWMS?) should be a priority—including automating tasks that keep directories relevant. A check-in system that updates hot desk occupancy, for example, means employees always know where to find co-workers—reducing confusion and unnecessary inquiries while increasing collaboration and productive communication.

4. Emergency delegation

An emergency is no time for chaos. In the event of a fire, inclement weather, or other disaster, an action plan prevails. Your employees should understand their responsibilities and how to act accordingly. Emergency delegation is centrally important among facilities management processes and procedures.

Start by naming emergency leaders—individuals responsible for critical tasks. Have standard operating procedures for these tasks, such as checklists or "if this, then that" actions. Then, develop a general situation-based plan for all emergencies. Where should employees exit in case of fire? What should they do during an active shooter situation? Where should they take cover in case of a tornado? Develop these processes in granular detail and make everyone aware of the appropriate actions. Then, quiz and drill everyone to ensure they're prepared for any eventuality.

5. Workplace analyses

Every facility manager needs a process for collecting, aggregating, analyzing, and presenting workplace data for better decision-making and growth. Data and analyses provides for dynamic understanding of workplace needs and trends.

Use an IWMS in conjunction with data collection tools, such as net promoter surveys or Internet of Things (IoT) devices. Make sure there's a method for collecting, categorizing, and ordering data. Then, ensure that data can be presented in a way that makes it easy to identify trends, anomalies, or demands. For example, occupancy sensors can send weekly room and desk occupancy data to your IWMS. The easier you make collecting and reviewing data, the more you'll know about your workplace.

Structure creates stability

Every workplace process you create adds structure. The more structure you have, the easier it is to shape the best possible workplace for your employees. Start with these five core processes. Good processes make it easier to adapt as your workplace grows and becomes more complex.

What is Strategic Facility Planning (SFP) and 4 steps to conquer it

The type, quantity and location are important to the SFP process, which encompasses understanding, analysing, planning and acting for the long term.

In order for FM providers to effectively address the needs of public sector organizations, it is imperative to move beyond Facility Management and engage in a degree of Strategic Facility Planning (SFP). SFP identifies the type, quantity and location of spaces required to fully support the organizations business initiatives and should be framed within the organization's vision.

SFP includes three primary components

An understanding of the organization's culture and core values and an analysis of how existing and new facilities must manifest that culture and core values within the physical space or support their change;

an in-depth analysis of existing facilities – including location, capability, utilization and condition;

and an achievable and affordable plan that translates the goals of the business plan into an appropriate facility response.

SFP described as a four-step process

1. Understanding: The thorough understanding the organisation's mission, vision, values, and goals;
2. Analysing: The analysis of the organization's facility needs;
3. Planning: The development of strategies that meet long-term needs of the organization;
4. Acting: The implementation of planned strategies.

As SFP merges with strategic policy objectives of each particular sector or organization, alignment among stakeholders is critical for successful partnerships. In this regard, there is a transcendence away from a one directional purchaser-supplier association to a more integrated and cooperative relationship.

An ongoing process

Accordingly, the process of strategic facility planning should be ongoing as facilities, real estate and infrastructure should be consistently evaluated. This ensures that public sector buildings and other real estate assets are optimized in a way that is best suited to match the vision, and to meet the policy objectives of the sector or organization. As such, the planning model requires a life-cycle analysis, which includes an evaluation of total ownership cost and life-cycle cost. This is in contrast to the relative value output of building assets in economic terms but social externalities as well.

What are your thoughts? Is Strategic Facility Planning something you are practicing in your organization now or are there barriers that limit the ability to use this approach? Share in the comments below!

About Service Futures

Service Futures represents the most important visions, trends and insights for the future of service, facility management, the workplace as an experience, HRM and outsourcing.

Across all our topics, we have one single goal; to enrich our readers with ideas and thoughts that help them become more courageous and creative in their work now and in the future. We do this based on thorough industry research, theory, practice and by engaging the foremost experts to express their visions and thoughts in the most influential way possible.

Building owners and operators who fail to embrace the insights within their buildings are being left behind. Their ability to manage costs, meet compliance requirements, satisfy occupants, and grow building equity compromised.

Speaking to attendees at IFMA, I outlined a six-step process for leveraging a 360-degree view of building data to improve results.

Step 1: Centralize all building data in a single platform that gives you a complete view of real-time and historical data.

Step 2: Benchmark your current and historical performance against peer data.

Step 3: Analyze your performance and set realistic goals for building performance.

Step 4: Make a two-year plan to improve performance in key areas that are important to your business, your occupants, and to your organization.

Step 5: Act on the plan. Stay informed with real time data, trend analysis and alerts that keep you on track to meet your goals.

Step 6: Measure, verify, and communicate your progress with standard dashboards and reports that keep everyone focused on the goals.

Facilities Management is all about coping with challenges. It's about assessing and responding to your building or facility's needs to maximise its smooth operation and efficiency. Whilst every facility has its own unique problems, challenges and solutions, there are a few overarching areas that, when paid attention to, can make a huge difference to your bottom line.

As energy costs and environmental concerns rise, sustainable facilities management has become a worldwide trend that cultivates good will, saves dollars for your building and, most importantly, reduces your building's carbon footprint.

With new technologies, the availability of government funding and significant returns on investment, going green has never been easier. Sustainable facilities management is applicable across the board, covering waste reduction and management, reduction of energy consumption and the use of greener energy sources.

In a 2007 survey of over 1500 facility management professionals, the majority of respondents reported spending significant amounts of time managing their facilities' environmental issues.*

Outsourcing expands your capabilities instantly with a team of experts often just a phone-call away. Choosing the right vendors and continually assessing their performance is a difficult but important task. Sticking with "˜the one you know', whilst convenient, doesn't always pay, so it's important to be constantly re-assessing your existing vendors.

To keep track of your vendors' prices and performance, good record-keeping and consistent evaluation is key. We recommend that facilities managers:

Research, record and compare vendor prices and information
Maintain searchable records of suitable vendors for future reference
Conduct regular vendor performance assessments.

Extend the life of your existing assets

In our fast-paced world of evolving technology, there seems to be a relentless push towards replacing assets more and more readily. Extending the life of your existing assets may not always be the sexiest option, but in many cases it's likely to be the most cost-effective (not to mention environmentally friendly).

The key to getting the most out of your investments is considered preventative maintenance. Think of it like a dental check-up. It may cost a small amount up-front, but it could save you a whole lot of trouble later on.

Smart assets management includes:

Comparing preventative and repair costs on all of your assets
Keeping good repair records to inform predictive maintenance schedules
Identifying and paying particular attention to mission-critical equipment.

Capture and use your data

Capturing accurate and reliable data is crucial to monitoring energy and resource usage and making informed, strategic decisions. Real-time data can help inform the operational side of business, helping facilities managers keep track of contractors, repair jobs and more. Key aspects of successful data management include:

Using historical repair data to inform repair or replace decisions
Monitoring real-time data on essential repair work
Comparing usage and spending trends to target wastage.

Avoid unnecessary costs

Keeping an eye on costs across the board can make all the difference to your bottom line. Facilities managers can make huge savings by:

Reducing non-urgent service calls
Keeping an eye on warranties
Working with fixed-cost vendors.

Stay up-to-date

Keeping on top of developments in the facilities management industry gives you access to the latest technologies and techniques in the business. Trade shows are a great way to stay informed, with industry-specific and generalist shows visiting Australian capital cities year-round.

Facilities management refers to the processes used to maintain and manage the facilities used by an organization during the day to day running's of the business.

Over the last few years more businesses have been starting to realize just how important effective facilities management can be for their profit margins. Facilities management teams are made up of professionals qualified in monitoring, maintaining, analyzing, repairing, and maintaining all facilities used to build and run a business including buildings such as warehouses and office blocks, staff, and human resources.

A facilities management team should also be active in devising and adjusting facilities management strategies to improve cost cutting and increase employee productivity.

A growing organization attracts a burgeoning list of resources to manage, including extra staff, HR, buildings, infrastructure, and equipment. The management team not only need to maintain the facilities, they also need to ensure all areas are compliant with health and safety regulations.

When a business is responsible for the health and wellbeing of so many employees the facilities management team needs to be ready to tackle any situation, so they can plan and respond immediately should changes or adjustments be needed, and handle on-site emergencies.

Listed below are just a few of the responsibilities a facilities management team focuses on to ensure smooth business operations:

- Risk assessment
- Waste management and disposal
- Access for disabled employees and members of the public
- Ensure compliance with all health and safety regulations
- Strategic planning
- Controlling the distribution and use of hazardous substances

When you realize that this is but a small sample of proper facilities management it becomes clear that a facility management program becomes an essential part any business. With today's technology this usually involves the use of tailor made software specific to the industry.

Facilities management allows a business to keep their finger on the pulse and properly co-ordinate timely maintenance of assets to ensure longer usability and reduce the total cost of ownership.

A business lacking the ability to effectively manage its facilities risks falling out of regulatory compliance, and may also find itself facing expensive repair bills, rather than relatively minor maintenance costs. There is also the danger mismanaged equipment can pose to both employees and the public.

As you can see, the facilities management team is an essential component of any business which can help improve cash flow and reduce waste. Small businesses lacking the resources to have a team on staff will find many affordable options

What are the benefits of facility management?

Just like many other facilities management companies, we're asked a number of questions on a daily basis by our clients. But one of the first they probably asked themselves is why they should outsource their facilities management services in the first place.

We thought we'd address this since there's likely to be an awful lot of businesses out there facing the same quandary. So here are the top benefits that we've seen businesses experience when they started outsourcing their facilities management.

COMPUTER-AIDED FACILITY MANAGEMENT (CAFM)

Traditionally, facilities management has been kept in-house for many businesses. But as technology has developed and improved, it's now easier and more efficient to outsource the services.

With an abundance of new devices like smartphones and tablets, the mobile maintenance apps offered by many facilities management companies mean that these services can be operated and the information accessed anywhere, anytime, whether you are working in the office, at home or on the move.

But instant access is just one of the benefits you can experience.

SAVING TIME & MONEY

Operating your facilities management in-house can eat into both working hours and profit.

By outsourcing, you can cut down on the amount of admin time staff are spending on the running of your facilities management. Leaving them to focus on core processes and the efficient running of the business.

Since in-house systems and software need to be regularly updated, which can often be expensive and time-consuming, you'll also save money in the long-term. Outsourcing will remove the cost and hassle of this.

An established business that uses their own engineers will have both the expertise and supply chain to source other specialist contractors. Which means you'll save time on contract management and potentially reduce the costs involved too.

EXPERTISE & KNOWLEDGE

Outsourcing to a fully-vetted facilities management specialist means that you can be confident they'll get the job done to the highest standards. For consistency, experienced businesses will ensure that you only ever deal with a single point of contact.

Using their knowledge and ability, they will be able to attract and retain the best personnel in the office and the best engineers on the ground. Applying best practice and adopting the latest service enhancements, they'll ensure that all work maintains compliance in the complex world of FM.

Rather than allocating your own time on managing the time and resources involved, outsourcing can help to maintain standards, mitigate risk and provide accurate reporting.

FLEXIBLE & ADAPTABLE

While companies evolve and grow, in-house facilities management systems can sometimes languish and get bogged down in the same processes.

Well-organised outsourced facilities management can offer the flexibility you need to meet changing requirements. As your business grows, you can pick and choose the services you need.

This not only means that your FM will always be relevant but also allows you to avoid any unnecessary costs for software upgrades or training.

EASY ACCESS

Making sure that people can access your facilities management systems easily is vital.

This doesn't just mean logging in quickly or remotely, it also relates to being able to allow multiple users access.

Having all of your data and systems in one location makes it easier to access information quickly and efficiently.

MEASURING, MONITORING & EVALUATING

KPI performance monitoring is often seen as a vital aspect of ensuring that the facilities management systems you have in place are working efficiently. Some facilities management companies are beginning to realise that the devil really is in the detail and are beginning to measure what the end user actually needs and wants, as opposed to simply measuring cost, quality and first-time fix.

Using the software of an outsourced FM company means that you can set, evaluate and, where needed, adapt targets and goals to be more effective.

This will also help when reporting to superiors on your facilities management objectives and achievements.

Top Five Benefits of Facilities Management

For a business to run effectively, every cog needs to provide support. But the larger and more complex your workplace becomes, the more cogs there are to manage. It's the role of a facility manager to keep track of them all. The benefits of facilities management are easy to see throughout the business—from the balance sheet to the company culture.

Overseeing workplaces gives facility managers plenty of insight into opportunities and inefficiencies. Take a look at the biggest benefits of good facilities management and how they help a workplace run at maximum efficiency.

1. Asset tracking and management

Tracking assets and budgets through spreadsheets is about as convoluted as it gets.

Take something like determining the cost per year of a copy machine. Here's a snapshot of how you might've figured this out before modern Integrated Workplace Management Systems (IWMS) or Enterprise Asset Management (EAM) platforms:

Look up annual maintenance logs
Compare maintenance logs to invoices
Review purchase orders for copier supplies

In this example, there's three different spreadsheets or document archives to search through—all to ballpark the annual operating cost of a single asset.

Today, there's a better way. Using an IWMS (read more on what is IWMS) or EAM platform, top-down asset management is efficient and easy. Repairs, maintenance, supplies, and other costs are coded to a specific cost center. The system provides instant insight no matter what's being measured.

2. Space optimization

Your lease may be 4,200ft2, but how much of that are you actually using? One of the biggest benefits of facility management software is knowing what you're actually getting for your money and how to make the most of it.

Let's say you're only using 3,200ft2. That's 1,000ft2 going to waste. Facility managers can look at data to figure out A) why that space isn't being used; and B) what it might be purposed for. FM data outlines the best way to recoup your cost per square foot and capitalize on it to improve revenue.

There's also the opposite situation to consider. If you're using 4,000ft2 and the walls are closing in, should you upgrade to a larger space or repurpose your current floor plan? Again, facilities management data will show the way. Adopting a new floor plan or flexible desking solution may save you thousands each month, while giving you the extra capacity you need—all without upgrading your total square footage.

The physical workplace is your largest single overhead cost. Maximizing value is the difference between your facilities being a cost center and a competitive advantage.

3. System of record

Your facilities' needs evolve over time, making a system of record crucial in understanding and meeting these demands. Tracking historical costs, trends, and changes over time is one of the key benefits of facility management systems. Take a look at a few of the hundreds of data points a facility manager needs to track:

Space occupancy growth over time

Employee locations or assigned workstations

Asset costs and life cycles

Utility costs

Building repair and capital improvement costs

This small portion of data represents the ebb and flow of a workplace's needs, as well as those of the people within it. Understanding change over time helps with everything from budget planning, productivity analysis, and real estate forecasting. Well-managed data is at the center of accurately predicting effective facilities management.

4. Cost analysis

Cost governs everything in the workplace. Knowing how much something costs or what recurring costs your company faces is important, but these amounts are far from the total cost of operating a business.Facilities management analysis provides keen insight into the real costs of keeping your workplace running.

For example, knowing how much space you're effectively using versus the cost of your lease will show the real cost per square foot. From there, you can determine other outlays, like the cost per hot desk as opposed to utilization. Insights abound when you start looking at specific costs versus their contribution to the business.

Understanding and analyzing various workplace costs drives effective business planning. You'll know how much you spend annually on utilities. You'll be able to plan for expansion costs when the time comes to get a bigger office. And, you'll know how to properly budget something like IT service for the year.

5. Integration

Your workplace is getting smarter. The benefits of integrated facilities management support a growing office Internet of Things (IoT). Investing in and managing connected devices is a recipe for even better facilities management and decision-making.

Office IoT is a rapidly growing segment of facilities management. In many ways, it's also making facilities managers' jobs easier. Take something like an occupancy sensor. Installing one in every conference room can immediately signal if the room is occupied. Sensors provide insights without manual intervention. This is the case for most integrated, automated technologies...but only if they're properly integrated and well-managed. Facility managers play an essential role in making the most of the IoT.

Culminating in a better workplace

Each of these benefits contributes to a workplace that's well-run, efficient, and productive. Through proactive facilities management, business executives know more about the most important part of the company: the workplace. And with that insight comes the ability to make better decisions about how to improve it.

Definitions of Facilities Management

There are many varying definitions of facilities management. The British Institute of Facilities Management perceives it as "the integration of processes within an organisation to maintain and develop the agreed services which support and improve the effectiveness of its primary activities" (BIFM, 2010) Price describes facilities management as an integrated approach to operating, maintaining, improving and adapting the buildings and infrastructure of an organisation in order to create an environment that strongly supports the primary objectives of that organisation (Price, 2000; Baldry, 2008) The facilities management movement can be summarized as a belief in potential to improve processes by which workplaces can be managed to inspire people to give of their best, to support their effectiveness and ultimately to make a positive contribution to economic growth and organizational success. (Alexander, 1994)

The Role of Facilities Management

The role of facilities management is gaining recognition within the economy. Government policies in a market economy, such as competitive policies, deregulation and privatisation, have each had an influence on the growth of facilities management over the years. In the Japanese economy, facilities management is already considered as a key element for economic success. They place a greater importance on office productivity and therefore facilities management is seen as a way of improving the efficiency of office workers in Japan. (Alexander, 1994)

Alexander, (1994) says that the role of facilities management should be defined by the relationship of facilities to the core business of an organisation in which success is measured by the degree and quality of support they provide to achieving key business objectives or goals. The role and responsibility of facilities management will vary in different organisations. Selecting the correct role of facilities management is critical to the success and effectiveness of an organisation. Creating a facilities management profile based on a case specific basis should potentially lead to successful facilities management practice.

The growing pressures of the competitive business world have made organisations realise that they must gain some form of competitive advantage from every section of their organisation. This must also include the costs of running the working environment. In these organisations, facilities are no longer allocated insignificant time but the strategic role of facilities management is widely recognised as well as the benefits of effective management (Baldry, 2008). In the past businesses were operating within a fairly stable economic environment. However the evolution of technology, cost of space, global competition and the greater impact of making mistakes has forced organisations to manage their resources effectively. This issue has given rise and placed more importance on the concept of facilities management. The biggest challenge facilities managers come across is the management of resources in a rapid and constantly changing environment. (Barrett, 1998)

As Alexander (1996), emphasizes, the role that facilities management plays in its contribution to the success of the organisation has gained increasing importance since the start of the facilities management concept. Initially facilities management was managed as an isolated activity and considered as an expense like any other cost within a business. Now facilities management is managed as an integrated activity, with the commercial, manufacturing and marketing function of the organisation. Facilities management has bought to the surface many opportunities to gain a competitive advantage over your competitors. Therefore, it seeks organisational effectiveness to help organisations to allocate their resources in a way that allows them to flourish in the very competitive markets. This has therefore encouraged management and business owners to realise that for organisations to benefit from their huge investment in facilities, they have to manage them actively and creatively, with commitment and a broader vision (Amaratunga, 2001)

The Centre for Facilities Management (CFM) describes facilities management as “the process by which an organisation delivers and sustains a quality working environment and delivers quality support services to meet the organisation’s objectives at best cost” It is accepted that facilities management covers a wide range of services and the success or partial failure of an organisations business is dependent on the management of those services

(Chotipanich, 2004). Such services can include property management, financial management, change management, human resources management, health and safety management, in addition to services such as building maintenance, domestic services (cleaning and security) and utilities supplies. The essence of facilities management lies in the ways in which facilities are adjusted to business needs and in the effectiveness of the systems that ensure non-core activities deliver value for money (CFM, 1992).

At a national level, the strategic objective of facility management is to provide better infrastructure and logistic support to businesses of all kinds and across all sectors. At a local level, its objective is the effective management of facility resources and services in providing of support to the operations of organisations, their working groups, project teams and individuals (Nutt, 2000). Therefore, according to Nutt (2000), the primary function of facilities management is resource management, at strategic and operational levels of support.

McNaughton 2007 says "Facilities management provides an opportunity for businesses and large conglomerates to focus on their "core business" leaving the secondary services of security, mailing and cleaning in the hands of the facilities management experts". If implemented correctly, facilities management can benefit your company in the following ways:

Reduced risk and increased productivity

Reduced operating costs by focusing on core business structures

Encourages and sustains a healthy and safe corporate culture

Delivers sustainable resource utilisation

Optimise asset utilisation

Operational and Strategic Facilities Management

Facilities management can be divided into two sections, namely operational facilities management and strategic facilities management. Operational facilities management is the interaction within the facilities department itself (i.e the facilities manager and the various functional units such as maintenance, interior planning, architecture etc). The various functional units can be in house or outsourced. Each functional unit should be aware of current techniques and regulations within their specific area of work. The facilities manger is expected to communicate with the core business regularly to identify current facilities requirements. The facilities manager will then benchmark facilities service currently in practice within the organisation against other facilities management organisations and see where an improvement can be made (Barrett, 1998). It can be said that the primary function of facilities management is the operational side as it is the most visible. The function supports the regular needs of the core business. (Chotipanich, 2004)

Strategic facilities management looks at the future. The facilities manager will interact with the core business to establish future changes that might occur to the business due to external factors such as competitors etc. The facilities manager will also identify possible developments within the facilities management arena. Interaction between strategic and operational facilities management must occur and the aim is to synergistically balance current operations with the needs of the future. (Barrett, 1998)

The figure above (Barrett, 1995) is a generic facilities management model developed by Barrett. It clearly shows the different relationships and communication lines as well as the difference between operational and strategic facilities management. The separation of the core business and facilities management is clear in the above diagram and this emphasises the fact that facilities management is only beneficial if it supports the primary business objectives. It also distinguishes between the current and future environment and makes it easier to understand how facilities management is conducted. Linkages 1, 2 and 3 are at an operational level and 4, 5 and 6 are at a strategic level.

The structure of facilities management is related to the needs, environment and circumstances of the organisation at the time. Its practice and composition are particularly important to the characteristics and contexts of the organisation. (Chotipanich,

2004)

Barrett (1998) suggests that facility managers should not just select service items from the standard list at random, but provide only those services that are needed by their particular organisation. Facilities management practice is seen as adapting to its situation. Barrett (1998) also stands by the fact that facilities management practice needs to be personalised to a specific organisation.

The facilities managers are involved in strategic planning i.e plans for the future as well as daily operations, particularly in relation to buildings and premises. Responsibilities and duties may vary depending on the type of corporation but the most likely responsibilities include:

contract management

procurement management

maintenance of the grounds and buildings

general cleaning of the facility and refuse disposal

catering and vending

health and safety

security

utilities and communications infrastructure

Facilities management is a very important concept in this competitive business world. If this concept is not managed correctly or neglected, it will be to the detriment of your organisation. In the past businesses were operating in a stable economic environment and as a result the setting of goals were done and not redone for a considerable amount of time. In this current economic state, the goals of organisations often change as the economic environment presents new challenges. The increase in competition, employee expectations and the changes in technology forces businesses to manage their resources effectively to stay profitable.

What are the benefits of facility management outsourcing?

What are the benefits of facility management outsourcing and what to consider before taking the final decision? Here are the key considerations you have to make!

The sentiment toward outsourcing is changing heavily. Whereas companies in the late 2000's focused on insourcing, as a response to changes in political sentiment, wage deflation, and high labour supply, the reality today signals a net increase in outsourcing consumption. When evaluating the risks and benefits of outsourcing, customers no longer reach the conclusion of bringing services back in the house. Instead and as Deloitte puts it in their latest Global Outsourcing Survey; "Companies are broadening their approach to outsourcing as they begin to view it as more than a simple cost-cutting play."

The key benefits of outsourcing

Successful and well-organized outsourcing can grow profitability, improve productivity, reduce business risks, grow competitiveness and let companies focus their efforts on their core business and key competitive advantage.

Most times, tasks are outsourced to vendors who are specialized in their field of business and have better expertise with non-core business processes than the ones at the outsourcing organization. Naturally, expertise and experience in completing tasks often results in a better quality output and tasks can be completed faster and more effectively.

Imagine you are managing a company that produces apple juice. You are most likely an expert in the production methods and processes specific to this product. Things like managing your facilities, improving IT systems or HR fall outside of these specific core competencies. In this case, you might gain a strategic advantage in outsourcing these tasks to specialists that can handle these tasks more efficiently and have the expertise necessary to take your company in the right direction.

Factors to consider when outsourcing

Even though outsourcing comes with many benefits, following factors and considerations should be made before taking a final decision.

Factors to consider when outsourcing

Is there a competitive advantage of doing the task in-house?

If you're not a tech company, then it may not be necessary to have an internal IT department. As long as the task/service does not support your core product, outsourcing can be a cost-efficient and strategically wise option.

Does the task represent a temporary or recurring need?

Does the task represent a temporary need or a one-time event? Then outsourcing the task to a third party, who has the expertise and can deliver a professional quality output can be a better option than hiring a new team of people that possess the skills you desire.

Can the task be handled more efficiently (with regard to knowledge, costs) externally?

Referring to, what previously has been mentioned - expertise and experience in completing tasks often result in a better quality output and tasks can be completed faster and more effectively.

Are the costs of the service lower than what it would cost in time and manpower to do in-house?

Naturally, if a third party can fulfil the task with a better output and for a lower cost than what you can do internally - outsourcing can be a great way to improve your balance sheet.

Besides clarifying those questions, you also need to set your expectations for a potential outsourcing relationship. Would you feel more comfortable with a conventional transaction-based approach which keeps you and your outsourcing vendor abstracted to the extent of your contracted agreements? Or would you prefer to adopt a Vested Outsourcing Approach that is highly collaborative and enables true win-win relationships in which both parties are equally committed to each other's success?

There are many considerations and clarifications to make before taking the final outsourcing decision and finding just the right outsourcing partner. When it comes down to everything, all that counts is what you and your managing partners believe it takes to continue winning in today's rapidly changing environment.

Adding Value: How Facility Managers Contribute to the Bottom Line

The biggest construction project today is not an office tower, a school or a hospital. Although work is well under way, there was no formal groundbreaking ceremony. Nor are there blueprints or models to indicate the final form of what's being built. On the contrary, work will likely never be complete. That's because what's on the drawing board is a new role for facility executives.

Identifying characteristics of that new role was the focus of six months of research by the editorial staff of Building Operating Management magazine. Titled "Tomorrow's Facility Executive -- Today," the project involved teleconferences, roundtable discussions and phone interviews with 77 leading facility executives in corporations, health care organizations and educational institutions at the K-12 and college and university levels. The result amounts to a punch list for facility executives interested in how to tackle challenges in the industry.

Why do facility executives need a new place in the corporate hierarchy? The reason is as easy to state as it can be difficult to accomplish: to use facilities to add value to organizations.

Given the amount that organizations invest in physical assets, the onus is on the facility executive to pay heed to the direct impact facilities have on the bottom line. But reducing expenses isn't the only challenge facing organizations -- or facility executives.

Increases in productivity offer an opportunity to boost long-term profitability in a way that the most aggressive cost-cutting can't match. Companies must satisfy customers to remain competitive. Rapid changes in the business environment have increased the importance of innovation, flexibility and time to market. Attracting and retaining qualified employees is a top priority for some organizations; for some, uptime is high on the agenda. The physical environment can help organizations achieve those goals and others.

As with anything involving facilities, the effort to create a new role for facility executives is best seen as a long-term project. Some facility executives have been going about that task for years. In the eyes of some of their peers, who are now beginning the effort, those early starters might seem to be lucky to have found organizations where management is willing to listen to facility executives. The reality is that very few organizations start out "enlightened." Getting the light bulb to go on in the mind of a CEO or CFO almost always takes time, hard work and good ideas.

The good ideas uncovered by the research paint a picture of how to become "Tomorrow's Facility Executive -- Today." This issue marks the start of a series of articles based on that research, articles that will examine key strategies for adding value to organizations. The pieces in this issue examine the question of how to identify real value in an organization. Future issues will cover such topics as how to use numbers effectively, how to develop communication strategies and how to build relationships.

Understand Top Management's View of Value

Imagine a facility executive trading places with a CEO for a day. The CEO would have to field complaints about a roof leak or find out what it's like to have phone calls go unreturned. Meanwhile, ensconced in the top executive's chair, the facility executive would scour the budget for money to replace that roof -- unless, that is, there was a board meeting to consummate a merger, or a hastily convened session to deal with a product recall, or any of the other things that keep the CEO from focusing on facilities.

Rather than wishing that the CEO would walk a mile in their shoes, the most successful facility executives do the opposite: They lace up an imaginary pair of the CEO's wingtips and try to understand what top management expects of facilities.

What they see varies dramatically from organization to organization. But there is one constant: cost control. "It's what they pay you to do," said one facility executive.

In one form or another, money is cited as the biggest challenge in the effort to add value to an organization. Top management in one Fortune 500 company wants facilities to reflect the status of the corporation, a leader in its field. Still, said the facility executive, management keeps asking the same question about facilities: "Why does it cost what it does to do what we do?"

At one university, the top facility executive is on good terms with top managers and with deans. "Financial processes at the university bring us together. No one hesitates to pick up the phone." But that does not mean he's on easy street. "It wouldn't be facilities if we weren't scrapping for resources."

What complicates the challenge of adding value is that cost control isn't enough. Facility executives must be able to deliver the right level of facility performance in key areas, whether the measure is comfort, uptime for critical facilities, the appropriateness of the work environment or real estate transactions. If limited resources make that impossible, facility executives should warn top management where performance may fall short.

A good litmus test of top management's expectations for facilities is the question of whether facilities are seen as a burden. "The closer you get to the CFO, the more that term applies," said one facility executive who has held senior positions in several large organizations where cost reduction was a major priority.

More often than not, however, facility executives rejected the term burden. "I wouldn't say management considers facilities a burden," said one facility executive. "They consider them a major part of our business. But we are continually being pressed to cut costs."

"Our management and board have a balanced view," said another facility executive. "They see that facilities bring a lot of value. But they also bring a lot of cost."

That balanced view is shared by successful facility executives. They have a solid grasp of what one facility executive called "the business of the business" and use organizational goals as the touchstone for facility decisions. That's true whether facilities are seen as a burden or not.

"In a market-driven company, the focus is always on the market," said a facility executive who has worked for several Fortune 500 firms. "Facilities and operations are a small part of the picture."

Align Facility Plans with Business Goals

When facilities are seen as a burden, success in facility management may come down to making lemonade out of some pretty sour lemons.

Consider the facility executive at a large urban hospital. Call it Hospital A. Across town, management at Hospital B has invested millions of dollars over a decade and a half to build a replacement hospital, a rehab hospital, medical office buildings and other new facilities; top executives rank physical assets second only to staff in value to the organization.

The attitude of senior executives at Hospital A could not be more different. They point to data showing that facilities don't really matter to patients. It's the hospital's medical staff and technology that count. That's the facility executive's cue: "This is going to sound awful, out of context: The patients don't matter. I've got to keep the doctors and nurses happy. If they're happy, they're going to take care of the patients."

That's not to say the facility executive is happy. It drives him crazy to see repairs put off so long they turn into capital expenditures. But he realizes that his best argument for funding is that facilities can help recruit and retain medical staff, not that the physical environment will pull in more patients.

Aligning with the strategy of the organization is a basic approach that can be overlooked by facility executives frustrated because top management so often turns down requests for funds. But supporting corporate strategy doesn't necessarily mean slashing expenses. "While real estate is a cost and management is concerned about it, they are also concerned about productivity and providing a cost-effective, efficient, safe, pleasant place to work," said one facility executive. "Our challenge is delivering that within a reasonable cost framework."

Facility executives should be alert to changing external conditions that alter company strategies. Competition for fee-for-service patients, for example, has led some health care organizations to see facilities as a way to attract customers. The power outage of August 2003 helped facility executives throughout the Northeast sell infrastructure improvements. One health care facility executive said that bankruptcies of other hospitals have shown top management the risk of letting the physical plant deteriorate so long that the organization simply can't afford to replace items when they finally wear out.

A facility executive in touch with management's ideas is more likely to spot ways to add value. About three years ago, one company decided to focus more directly on its core restaurant business. One goal was getting managers to spend more time in restaurants and less time in field offices. "Our department took that as a cue," said the company's facility executive. "We changed the concept of the traditional field office and made it a resource center." The resource centers were no longer workplaces for managers but rather locations to be visited or accessed electronically; average office size was cut by 60 percent.

Aligning with corporate strategy pays long-term dividends, said the facility executive. "This is an operations company. Facilities are not even secondary. We are off the radar screen in some cases. But when you show value, it snowballs. All of a sudden you gain momentum."

Identify Needs Facilities Can Address

No one will deny that a better looking campus will make a university more appealing to potential students. And common sense says that a well-designed workplace can boost productivity by improving communication, eliminating distractions or reducing absenteeism. But, for facility executives intent on adding value, no facility benefit is relevant, except one: the one that meets a specific organizational need.

A good example is speed. Getting a high school renovation completed in June rather than July isn't likely to be as important to the school board as getting a new branch open sooner is to bank management.

"We call it time to market," said a facility executive from a financial institution. "If four banks are going in at an intersection, and you're the last one, you have to take customers from the other banks. Time truly is money."

When speed matters, companies will make investments to enable them to move faster. One very profitable organization has a 100 percent annual churn rate. "We control churn by supplying commodity spaces and standardizing workstations and the technology the supports the business," said the facility executive. "Everything is race-wired. Everything is cabled to allow for a quick-connect. Lighting is built on a 5-by-5 grid. We can move a thousand people over a weekend if we don't have to paint and spackle." Lower long-term costs aren't the only benefit of speed that has caught the attention of top executives. "We've been told that we're a strategic advantage," said one facility executive. "Together with our IT department, we can position our products faster than our competitors." As a result, the company is willing to accept higher initial costs.

The extent to which the link between organizational need and facility benefit can be quantified varies. For example, increasing reliability for data centers increases cost, but the payback can be gauged by the additional amount of uptime it brings. Update an old branch bank that still has avocado and harvest gold as its color motif, or customize a retail outlet to appeal to a demographic group, and the return shows up in increased business.

But not all investments in aesthetics can be measured so easily. "You've got to have really good facilities to attract students," said the facility executive at one university. "They have much higher expectations." But quantifying the value of a positive first impression is difficult. Schools can query students about the physical environment, just as hospitals can ask patients how happy they were with the facilities, but customer satisfaction surveys can't directly measure financial returns on an investment in facilities. It's ultimately a judgment call whether the investment is worthwhile. Cost matters but the perceived need for a better image determines how much expense is appropriate.

Recruitment and retention are other areas where facilities can have an impact. One hospital recently opened a state-of-the-art intensive care unit. "All we have to do is get the nurses in the door," said the facility executive. "As soon as they see it, they're here. They don't care who the doctors and other nurses are -- at least for a while." In another hospital, nursing vacancies dropped nearly 90 percent with the move into a replacement facility.

It's not just in tight labor markets that a facility has value as a tool for recruitment and retention. One organization concluded that limiting call center employees to 3-by-3 foot cubicles caused too much turnover. Another facility executive recalled moving a call center out of "a dog of a facility" and into smaller but nicer space with more amenities. "The better facility definitely translated into less turnover," he said. Front-line supervisors in the call centers remained the same.

Despite cases like that, demonstrating how much impact facilities have on recruitment and retention is often difficult. "I don't think I've ever heard of anyone going into an exit interview and saying they were leaving because the facilities were bad," said one facility executive. "When turnover is high, the facility is just one more thing to look at." Absent a specific need, it's often tough to convince management to invest extra in facilities to help attract and keep employees.

Balanced View

When it comes to adding value, a balanced perspective is the hallmark of successful facility executives. These facility executives bring a skeptical eye to the question of whether, and to what extent, benefits can be quantified.

A hard-nosed mindset is often evident in discussions about the direct impact facilities can have on employee productivity. Most facility executives believe the physical environment can impede performance. "I don't know if I can improve test scores," said one facility executive. “But I’m sure I can make them go down.” What’s more, if productivity is defined as helping to recruit or retain employees, or to maintain uptime, then facilities may be acknowledged as playing a major role.

But on the question of whether facilities help improve the performance of people who use a space, opinions vary widely. Many studies have claimed to prove that facility improvements can increase productivity, but taken as a whole that body of research has significant flaws. Some studies depend entirely on subjective indicators of productivity. In other cases it’s impossible to rule out other, non-facility factors that could account for any gains in productivity.

The health care industry has embarked on an ambitious effort to make the connection between elements of facility design and specific outcomes. Known as evidence-based design, the strategy sets specific targets and then measures the impact of facilities on achieving those aims. For example, the goal might be reducing the number of infections that patients acquire in the hospital; a design strategy to address that problem might be the use of private rooms.

Could an evidence-based design approach work for other industries? One obstacle is the difficulty of measuring white collar productivity at all. The more that a job is repetitive, the easier it is to measure productivity. It’s much harder to quantify how productive a knowledge worker is. Either way, it’s difficult to isolate the impact of a specific factor, like the physical environment.

Some organizations do accept the idea that facilities are an important tool to boost employee performance. One company outsources most facility and real estate functions but supports an in-house real estate research department that explores ways to improve the workplace. Other corporations have used a change in the physical environment to help drive a change in the corporate culture. They saw the facility as a way to address an organizational need -- even if the impact could not be quantified easily.

Customer Satisfaction

Linking need and facility benefit can be a complicated matter. A case is point is the Press Ganey patient survey, a tool widely used in health care to rate customer satisfaction. Some of the questions relate directly to the physical environment. And new or upgraded space often receives much higher marks. That makes Press Ganey scores potentially valuable evidence for justifying investments in facilities. "If you're successful in making a link between Press Ganey and the condition of the facilities, you've won a big battle," said one facility executive.

But a closer look reveals a more complex picture. For one thing, any big jump in scores on facility measures is often short lived. "Within a year, it comes almost back down to the original level," said one facility executive.

What's more, it's not the facilities themselves that count most with patients. Facilities actually land near the bottom on the scale of things patients rank as most important.

A facility executive focused on fluctuating Press Ganey scores might miss other opportunities. One hospital upgraded its cafeteria but saw little change in patient satisfaction scores. That was a disappointment to the facility executive until he realized employee satisfaction had jumped, an important consideration given the tight market for qualified medical staff.

Although it's often helpful to quantify the benefits of a facility can offer, that may not be necessary when the need is a high priority. One organization was considering a consolidation that would have moved employees into Class A space not far from the existing location. The savings were significant. "From the cost perspective it was a slam dunk," the facility executive said. What's more, the new location meant a shorter average commute for employees. But the move never happened. The old facility was essentially next door to a major customer. Location amounted to a key competitive advantage. Moving even a few miles away, the business unit concluded, would have jeopardized its relationship with the customer. "We decided there was more opportunity to grow the business if we stayed in the existing location," said the facility executive.

Four Main Functions of Facilities Management

The broad scope of facilities management makes it a hard position to define. Where a Sales Manager is directly responsible for managing the performance of salespeople, the functions of facilities management go far beyond "managing facilities." As a result, it's often difficult for companies to maximize the advantages of a good facility manager.

But what is the importance of facilities management? To truly understand what a facility manager does, what they're responsible for, and what effect they have on a company, it's best to break down their scope of work. That means taking a closer look at the four main pillars of facilities management: People, processes, the building, and technology.

Supporting people

The foremost objective of a facility manager is creating an accommodating work environment for employees. This serves many broader goals, including attracting and retaining top talent, improving efficiency and productivity, and creating a positive workplace culture. Facility managers provide employee support in many ways, including:

Coordinating desking arrangements

Managing employee directories

Facilitating moves and space utilization

Handling emergency planning

Facility managers serve as a bridge between the workplace and the employees working within it. Whenever issues of accommodation, safety, or comfort arise, it's up to the facility manager to solve them.

This applies upward, as well. Facility managers are responsible for providing vital planning data to the C-suite and determining the long-term approach to workplace optimization. Their everyday interaction with the workplace sheds light on true costs and competitive advantages at the employee level.

Establishing processes

What are the functions of facilities management without a process to govern them? Establishing processes brings order to the workplace. Order creates a system of expectations, which breeds organization that positively impacts the way people utilize the workplace. The workplace runs on a multitude of processes, including:

Submitting a work order request
Reserving space within the facility
Checking in guests and visitors
Emergency action planning

Facility managers serve the dual role of identifying governance areas and adapting processes to cover them. Whenever a new situation arises, it's up to the facility manager to create order from chaos and building a repeatable framework for handling that scenario again in the future.

Developing processes is also where the scope of facility management expands its reach. New processes may involve different departments, employees, assets, fixtures, and spaces—all of which connect the many aspects of the business.

Facilities upkeep and improvement

As the name implies, facility management is largely rooted in facilities upkeep and improvement of the physical building. It's the most common answer when asked, "What does facility management include?"

But this is also the most robust scope of expectations for facility managers. It involves not only tending the building, but cultivating partnerships, future planning, and asset management. Some examples of this broad range of responsibilities include:

Finding and maintaining vendor contracts
Repair, maintenance, and building improvement
Workplace cleaning and décor
On- and off-site property management

If it has to do with the physical building, it falls within the facilities manager's realm. Facilities are the second largest expense behind the workforce—it's the job of a facility manager to turn the workplace into a competitive advantage, instead of a cost center. It's about ensuring facilities meet the needs of the people using them.

Technology integration

More important than ever is the need for facilities managers to understand and use technology. Workplace management systems aggregate data, which drives crucial decisions about how to run the business and shape the workplace. Identifying and implementing the right technology is a chief responsibility of facility managers.

Integrating physical technology typically falls on the IT department. However, facilities managers are the first and last word on how they're selected, used, and leveraged. Some examples of what this looks like in a modern setting include:

Researching IoT devices based on data collection needs
Integrating IoT devices into everyday facilities processes
Determining the cost, ROI, and advantage of smart technologies
Using aggregated data to better understand the workplace

Using an Integrated Workplace Management System (read more on what is IWMS software), facility managers can collect and analyze data from networked technologies to get insights about the workplace. This fuels better decision-making on how to optimize the work environment for the people using it.

It's important to note that not all office tech relies on data collection. Access control systems support safety, while automation tech streamlines processes. And while there's a data component to any networked device or software, the true benefit of most tech is in its function. It's up to facility managers to understand and leverage this function for optimal ROI.

Putting it all together for facilities management

Facility managers support workers directly and indirectly. They establish processes for order and organization. They're charged with upkeep and improvement of the facilities themselves. They create complex integrations to leverage data for success.

When you put these four functions together, they paint a picture of what facility managers really do. Broadly speaking, their focus is on optimizing the workplace to support every aspect of the business it touches. But on a deeper level, it's about giving the company a steady foundation for success.

Why is Facility Management Important for Productivity?

Facility Management (FM) is a multi-departmental business evidence-based management discipline and software productivity that focuses on efficiency efforts and long-term success in areas like real estate, operational finances, human resources, maintenance and information technology (IT). Generally speaking, anything having to do with a facility manager, business' facility or space and physical assets is part of facilities management and productivity growth, and it's easy to see why.

When it comes to productivity, having all these elements in order is an essential recipe for success. A business can't run properly when its facilities and physical assets aren't in working order. However, beyond that, a well-run FM program can be a key factor in facilitating productivity for individual employees on a day-to-day basis in the workplace.

A facilities management professional should be in charge of these operations to ensure improved productivity within the company by using the information from maintenance and daily operations reports to determine the best solution for any problems that may arise that can ultimately negatively affect productivity within the workplace.

Basic Productivity Considerations in Facility Management

From broken computers to burst pipes, there are plenty of facility-related issues, errors and accidents that can bring productivity to a grinding halt for any number of employees in an office. When there isn't a proper reporting system or chain of command for dealing with facilities-related issues, productivity is derailed not only for the employees directly affected by the issues but also for many of their colleagues, subordinates, counterparts and managers. Even simple problems like a broken desk chair that won't be replaced for two weeks due to bureaucratic slowdowns can have a ripple effect throughout the office.

But when businesses pay proper attention to FM, they make it easier to move past these inevitable breakdowns in functionality and get productivity back on track as soon as possible. An office space that functions properly in a structural sense is better placed to function properly in a work outcome capacity as well. While this is a not insignificant benefit to incorporating FM techniques or even creating an FM department, it's not the only way good facility, space and physical asset management can make efficient operations more common. Solving problems efficiently when they arise and giving employees a way to report these problems is a good first step, but it's not the only way to make productivity a major focus of FM efforts.

Dimensions of Digitalization of Facilities Management

There are four different dimensions concerning the digitalization of facilities management. Technology has fast become a vital element of business, and increased digitalization may pose new challenges for facility management.

End-to-End digital facility management services allow the customers or employees to interact with the business on a digital level and it is a safe and secure way to aid in improving employee management. Digitalizing the facilities management aspects of the business can provide updates that can be accessed in whatever location they are needed, at whatever time they are needed. For example, if there is an emergency maintenance issue that arises, the facility manager will receive this information quickly and be able to provide the business with updated resources to ensure that processes are maintained and functioning while being able to go from facility to facility to take care of any other potential issues as well.

Digitalization means an increase in productivity and tracking and assigning maintenance requests are easier to do and can be tracked in real time. It offers the maintenance management team the ability to prioritize maintenance issues based on their priority status so that the management team can accomplish what needs to be done right away while being able to track other issues as they come. The real-time data that digitalization allows can also help foster collaboration from other team members across all departments so that work orders are assigned and tackled efficiently and easily without having to disrupt any other processes.

Workplace productivity and retention will also see vast improvements because the facilities management, IT, and HR departments can all become integrated with the digital system in order to maximize each department's potential.

Energy and sustainability can be translated into reduced costs and improved savings which will show an immediate return on the investment. Finally, compliance management in regards to the FM can be effectively monitored including the preventative maintenance aspects of the company as well as strategic management, completion schedules and predicted costs of each job.

Digitalization does, however, include a small investment but the potential is there, and the ROI can increase productivity and find cost reductions which will take functionality to a new and improved level of strategic management.

Competencies of Facility Management

There are several core competencies concerning facility management. Some of these core competencies include communication, finance and business, human factors, leadership and strategy, operations and maintenance, quality, technology and property management.

Communication is one of the most important aspects of any type of management position. Effective communication can help increase the company's effectiveness and timing as well as the understanding of the processes that are involved concerning facilities management. Messages within a business need to be clear and concise and easy to understand. To achieve effective communication when sending out messages, be sure that the message is broken up into smaller sections and the purpose of the message is clearly defined.

Operations and maintenance are also critical elements of a successful facilities management system. In addition to the normal maintenance and procedures, the facilities manager will also be responsible for effectively allocating space, ensuring compliance with government regulations, and developing a continuity plan so that the business can quickly recover after an incident or problem.

Facilities management ensures that the business remains in operating order, the employees are safe, productivity is increased, and the workplace remains a friendly and inviting environment for both employees and clients.

Facility management software and other computer aided project management solutions are often employed as a way to help keep track of goals and helps everything run smoothly while being more manageable. Facility management software is a web-based solution to help reduce the costs of maintaining the facility, improve the flow of information throughout the departments, and boost operational efficiencies.

How Facility Management Relates to Human Resources

The people who work in an organization's facilities are also part of FM, which means that human resources (HR) concerns and FM concerns often overlap. As a matter of fact, HR professionals working for businesses with significant FM programs may find themselves working with the facilities department's employees and tools more often than you might assume. While FM doesn't necessarily deal with HR functions like dispute resolution, legal compliance or payroll concerns, it can relate to things like employee satisfaction and recruitment. Think of it this way: If you showed up for a job interview and the receptionist couldn't tell you whether your interviewer was in the office and where your interview was to be held, you wouldn't be very impressed with the business, would you? Similarly, no candidate wants to feel a sense of chaos when they walk into a prospective employer's office. FM can absolutely help to keep these parts of the recruiting process under control.

Beyond recruiting, the synergy of FM and HR functions can mean smoother day-to-day operations for employees in all departments and leadership levels. Considerations like desk assignments and even seemingly minor things like deciding who gets to use which conference room when might not have a huge impact on the grand scheme of business operations. However, on a micro scale, these matters can make a dramatic difference in the way individual employees experience life in the workplace, which, in turn, has an effect on how well they work and how much they produce.

Without the dual function of FM and HR in concert, these details can slip through the cracks as leadership in each individual department assumes that someone else in the organization is taking care of it. This kind of buck-passing is always detrimental to productivity, even when the focus of the task is something that seems like a relatively minor point of concern.

What FM Technology Means for HR Professionals

The old-school solution of using spreadsheets and other static tools for FM tasks is gone, and useful Computer-Aided Facility Management (CAFM) programs like SpaceIQ's workplace management software have taken their place, providing FM professionals and their colleagues in departments like HR the ability to use simple, user-friendly technology to quickly and efficiently carry out various facility-related tasks. This in—and of—itself is a major productivity breakthrough; downloading a PDF of data aggregated by a software program is a lot simpler than hand-copying selected results tracked down one by one in an analog ledger.

FM technology allows HR professionals to quickly take care of simpler job tasks like desk provisioning, leaving more room in the schedule to take care of other FM-related tasks such as employee satisfaction analysis. Efficiency is always good for productivity and on the HR side of FM, tech tools are key to facilitating quick completion of routine tasks. But that employee satisfaction analysis your HR team is performing with data collected by FM tools does more than just make HR's jobs run more smoothly. It can also increase overall job performance across the board on your team.

Exploring the Ways FM Can Increase Employee Comfort and Motivation

Why is an a facilities management system a productivity savior? It's all about data, reporting, analysis, and action. The right tools will make it easy for HR and other management staff to take a look at the conditions of their office environment, which itself has a significant impact on how workers feel in their workplace. That may sound too "touchy-feely" from an old-school business management perspective, but all evidence points to the fact that happy employees are well worth the investment.

It's a sensible approach, and while it's borne out by data, it's easy to see how employee comfort in the workplace can actually have a lot to do with how well workers are able to do their jobs. Spending each day in the office bundled up and shivering isn't exactly going to help an employee feel excited about showing up to work each day and the fact of the matter is that the pain of being cold is distracting. It makes good sense, then, to find a temperature that works for your office but the challenge there is that each employee tends to have their own ideal operating temperature.

Sensor integration can actually be a great way to address this issue from an FM strategy point of view. While, in theory, employees can just adjust the temperature in a conference room when they walk in, they'll have to remember to adjust it back down or up when they walk out of the room again in order to leave it in a better place for the next employee. Smart sensors installed in conference rooms and unassigned office space can recognize an individual employee and draw from an FM profile detailing their preferences to make immediate adjustments as soon as they enter or check

themselves into a room. Tools like this make FM an essential element in the quest to make employees feel comfortable and satisfied at work so they'll repay your considerate treatment with the best work they can possibly do.

The tools you select for this task are important, though. SpaceIQ has powerful analytical and reporting tools that allow for one-click

PDF generation. That in and of itself is a productivity win, but it's what's contained within those rapidly generated documents that are really important for long-term performance gains across the board. If you're experimenting with different office arrangements and workspace sharing approaches, using SpaceIQ throughout the process can give you the ability to track precise locations and conditions to measure against quarterly financial reports and other productivity data. The guesswork era is over in FM and HR. Now you can have cold, hard data to back up your decision making, allowing you to choose an objective best scenario for employee productivity.

Productivity-Focused Tools

A good Facility Management solution makes optimal productivity an easily achieved goal through the use of specific tools and functions for an entire enterprise to make use of. Ultimately, this means that the program provides relevancy across all tiers of an organization's leadership structure. Even entry-level employees can get plugged into the system and use it on a daily basis to make logistical and collaborative parts of their job easier, resulting in more time spent doing and less time spent taking care of administrative mundanities.

Space Utilization Visualization

The space utilization visualization components of a program lays out the floor plan of your office to scale, including desks and even seat markers designating where employees are currently sitting. It also shows you where there are empty seats in the office at any given time. This record of unassigned desks is useful for management, who can determine whether they're wasting money on overhead costs relating to space and physical asset management based on the ratio of unassigned desks to the workforce in the office at a given time. Having a high-level view of this tracked in the system—again, not requiring independent tracking effort from an employee—allows management to perform quick, productive analysis and take this information to higher-ups for decision-making that's backed by data and illustrative examples. This also allows for on-demand provisioning of reserved desks and workstations in agile workspaces that take an open, modern approach to seat assignments.

Systems Integrations

Having to click around between multiple different browser tabs or application client windows takes time out of everyone's day. These seconds add up to minutes and hours over time. As more and more useful systems get plugged into facility management programs, employee attention will be much less scattered, which is always best for productivity. Even the most dedicated, efficient workers find that splintering their focus can have a negative impact on how much actual work they get done in a day. Fewer programs mean fewer distractions and more beneficial work output in the long run.

Employee Profiles

As an organization grows, it becomes increasingly cumbersome to keep track of individual employees in both a general and literal sense. Employee profiles inside a Facility Management program allow everyone with access to the program to do both. You'll be able to onboard your new employees more quickly, which is something HR will certainly appreciate and, after the initial onboarding into the system is complete, you'll be able to see what workstation an employee is currently occupying or where they are in the office. This can be helpful not only for those times when one team member is trying to track down another in an expansive workplace but can also give you a better idea of where an employee does his or her best work.

For example, if you happen to notice that a team member seems to have her best ideas when she's in the lounge area of your office, you may want to see whether working from home a few days a week allows her to reach peak productivity. This kind of optimization is only possible when you have the kind of on-demand reporting and observational tools that a CAFM program has to offer.

Fostering Productivity with Tech

Tech developments are usually heralded as the best new solution for productivity but, as we all know, a program has to actually work as intended to really make a difference in how easy it is to complete a given task. A good CAFM solution takes a multifaceted approach to the very concept of productivity.

Learn more on what is CAFM?

To improve productivity, technology should increase workplace productivity, rather than distract people. The technology should provide the users with ease and flexibility that can also adapt the changing needs of the business. Technology applies to the overall infrastructure of the business down to the applications that are used as well as the phone systems.

The best technology is the technology that does not take a lot of time to set up and learn. It should also not require a lot of additional time to maintain. While it may work, the facilities management professional should analyze the available tech to determine if it is increasing productivity and providing the employees with a more comfortable and suitable working environment.

What is the International Facility Management Association?

The International Facility Management Association, otherwise known as IFMA, was founded in 1980 and is one of the most recognized associations for facility management professionals in the world, boasting over 24,000 members in over 104 countries worldwide.

The International Facility Management Association offers development through different credentialing programs and conducts research to strengthen the skills of facility management. They also produce industry-leading magazines and newsletters.

Facilities management is important for productivity, and the IMFA has come up with eleven core competencies concerning facilities management.

Communication, Quality, and Technology

Through communication efforts, the facilities management professional team can develop plans of communications to effectively deliver the proper messages and recommendations to the workers, the public, senior management and even the customers. The facility manager will also develop and oversee the application of standards for the business and review performance records including benchmarking, KPI's, service response times and other measurable events. This information can help devise a plan of strategy to further improve productivity and also measure the quality of the services that are given.

The facilities manager also has the responsibility of auditing and documenting compliance codes, regulations, and other policies and standards to ensure everything is being followed.

When workers in an organization feel that they are working in a positive environment with open communication standards, then you will see improved performance and increased productivity. There are many factors to consider regarding a facilities management system. Not only should the maintenance issues be addressed and the easy measurements of the input and output of energy, rent, and wages, a facilities manager should also consider disruptive workplace factors that could increase the negative input and dampen productivity.

Productivity Blockers

Several factors can cause loss of productivity. The loss of productivity can ultimately lead to lost time and resources. Many of these issues can be rectified with the employment of a designated facility manager that is trained in reducing wasted productivity.

Sometimes it is required to review the amount of equipment and machines you have in the facility as well as their placement. The number of printers, fax machines, and copiers you have and where they are located, for example, can play a leading role in limiting productivity within the facility. Are there enough printers to handle the increased traffic the facility may be experiencing? How far do the employees have to go to get to these machines?

The design and space allocation of the facility is a vital element of workplace productivity. It is best to ensure that all services and machines the employers utilize are within a good distance of the relative working area. An efficient layout will fix operational adjacencies and will ultimately maximize workplace productivity.

Examine the amount of workplace accidents that exist. The facility manager can determine if any additional safety training is needed to avoid losing productive workplace hours.

Communication and an employee's self-worth and value are also critical elements of workplace productivity. The facility manager ensures that proper communication is available so that the employees can effectively communicate with each other. Social interaction is also appreciated within the workplace environment and is essential for valued relationships among the employees and the customers alike. Facilities management can examine the meeting and conference rooms for functionality and effectiveness and consider an updated design if needed to promote a more open and inviting environment with improved telecommunication processes as well.

The facility manager should have the skill sets, knowledge and abilities that are required to effectively perform and ensure that operations and maintenance run smoothly and efficiently. Planning and scheduling are daily tasks a facilities manager is presented with to support the facilities operations.

Having a cloud-based facilities management program at the root of business operations will also ensure that you are equipped to evolve with the times and also thrive in an agile, unpredictable environment.

Daily Operations and Soft FM

According to the IFMA, Facility management is the practice of coordinating the physical workplace with the people that are employed there and the overall work of the organization. Principles of business are being integrated with factors such as administration, architecture, and behavioral and engineering sciences.

Soft facilities management is another aspect of FM that is essential to the success of the business. Soft facility management services are those services, or elective, that are geared more towards the people that work for the company. Soft services include electives such as window cleaning, general cleaning services, security, mail management, waste management and even catering. These services ensure a comfortable and secure environment for the employees, which can, in turn, lead to improved productivity.

Facility management professionals can conduct a Facilities Needs Assessment to help them determine which of the above services are needed and which may be unnecessary. To complete the assessment, the facilities manager will consider if the needs are sufficient or efficient and if the facility needs maintenance or duplicate services can be eliminated. Security and sustainability are also objectives and require organization and the delivery of the services by the facilities manager to make the workplace safer, more efficient, and compliant.

Hard FM services are those services that are a physical part of the facility and cannot be removed such as heating, lighting, plumbing, fire safety systems, air conditioning, and building maintenance. These services are required and are typically required by law to be available in the workplace.

Under the Workplace Regulations 1992 for health, safety, and welfare these are regulations that the facilities manager must always consider and ensure are properly maintained and remain in working order.

These daily operations and maintenance services are performed and overseen by the facility management professional, and they may also handle the responsibility of the maintenance staff, payroll, of the maintenance staff, and the budget available for these services.

Overall, facility management is important for workplace productivity because it is an easy and efficient way of managing and tracking all the vital information concerning how the business is operated and maintained. Without these services and the lead of a facilities manager, then the business can experience increased downtime due to maintenance issues, lower employee morale, and decreased productivity which can result in the loss of revenue and the additional costs of maintenance due to the operations and systems that were not being managed and examined.

Facility management software helps the company reduce space and maintenance costs while increasing the efficient use of their other assets, as well as increases productivity. Computer aided facility management is an effective solution that allows a facility manager to plan, execute, and monitor all activities. These activities include planned preventative maintenance involving the services, space and move management, asset management, standard services, and even long-term planning needs concerning these services and the budgets required to align with the needs of the business.

Computer aided facilities management can also reduce the amount of inaccuracies that are reported and can help provide the most up to date information that is available. All of these factors can lead to reduced costs and greater efficiency in the workplace as well as improved customer service.

The Role And Responsibilities Of Facilities Managers

Facility management include all complex operating activities such as grocery stores, auto shops, sports complexes, jails, office building, hospitals, hotels and all other revenue generating. Facility manager's job purpose to create an environment that encourages output, is pleasing to clients and consumers, and is efficient. Facility mangers include a wide range of function and support services. All staff, students and volunteers are responsible for ensuring that they work in a manner which is safe to themselves and to others and to comply with relevant requirements of guidance to the national standees and the University of health and safety department. All staff parent or cares volunteers and students are urged to read the nursery health and safety policy and relevant parts in the university health and safety policy.

Facility management:-

According to Alan M.Levitt, "a facility may be a space or an office or suite of offices; a floor or group of floors within a building; a single building or a group of buildings or structures. These structures may be in an urban setting or freestanding in a suburban or rural setting. The structures or buildings may be a part of a complex or office park or campus."(Disaster Planning and

Recovery: A Guide for Facility Professionals.)
Total facilities management:-

Total facilities management include those things which everything needed such as services for living, working, healthcare, education, commercial development, retailing, and transportation and communication undertakings.

According to steven M.Price "facilities professionals are being asked to contain costs while achieving maximum beneficial use- that is, to achieve more withless."

Some other person describe to facility as a physical place where done business activities. Facility management duty to make plans according to business activity needs and demands .as a good facility management deal with those needs in the best and cost effective ways possible. Which responsibility play by facility managers explain below:-

Observe efficiency of organization

Make sure that the divergent processes, procedures, and standards present in a business complement rather than interfere with one another.

Observe all feature of facility maintenance

Tracking and responding to environmental, health, safety, and security issues.

Ensuring facility compliance with relevant regulatory codes and regulations

Educating the work force about all manner of standards and procedures, from ordering office supplies to acting in the event of a disaster.

The role and responsibilities of facilities managers:-

A facilities manager has a range of responsibilities including overseeing the daily running of a building and reducing its operating costs. In any organization facility manager is responsible for services of management which support business. Facilities mangers manage the continual maintenance of the building, identifying health and safety issues to make sure the building is safe for use and general responsibility for utilities, services and daily logistical management. A facilities manger also responsible for managing catering and cleaning services and utilising space management throughout the building.

Facility managers responsible for directing a maintenance staff.

Facility manager's duties related to standard maintenance, mailroom, and security activities, he or she may also be responsible for providing engineering and architectural services, hiring subcontractors, maintaining computer and telecommunications systems, and even buying, selling, or leasing real estate or office space.

The managers are also responsible for considering federal, state and local regulations.

Facility mangers also integrate knowledge workers into dynamic business environment of global competition, technological developments, security threats and changing values.

Scope of facilities management:-

Facilities management describe those core business activities where business are working and provide a good career path with the associated motivation that it brings. Good facilities management always try to introduce new idea and knowledge for improve standard, improve the consumer primary activities and protect the associated investments. Those by the scope of facilities management is wide and varied such activities which are include security, cleaning, maintenance, catering, landscaping, hygiene etc. Today the role and scope of facilities management have changed dramatically

Corporate social responsibity:-

Total corporate social responsibility can be subdivided into four primary criteria-economic, legal, ethical and discretionary responsibilities. Mark S.Schwartz and Archie B.Carroll, "Corporate Social Responsibility: A Three Domain Approach," Business Ethics Quarterly 13, no.4 (2003), 503-530; and Archie B.Carroll, "A Three -Dimensional Conceptual Model of Corporate Performance," Academy of Management Review 4(1979), 497-505.

These four criteria fit together to form the whole of a company's social responsiveness. Managers and organizations are involved in several issues at the same time, and a company's ethical and discretionary responsibilities are increasingly considered as important as an economic and legal issue.

Business ethics are moral principles that guide the way a business behave. Acting in an ethical way involves a distinguishing 'right' and wrong and then making the right choice. For example, policy with regard to honesty, health and safety and corrupt practice.

Facilities management also supporting the board to bring aspects critical to the facility management operational activities such as premises, local community and staff welfare. Facilities managers play a vital role to delivery of more facility by a number of stages in the life cycle of a building.

Today, facilities management challenges are integrating the resource with the user needs. Lavy (2008)conclude that facility management not only improve physical performance but also increase the satisfaction that the users feel while staying/working/teaching/learning in that building. It is important for facilities manager to understand the link between the institution aims and objective and the various group in the institution. The interface has to be strong and without it is easy to fail to work in the same direction (Housel, 1997). Therefore, a facility manager have to take account the needs of the users as basis for providing them with a suitable facilities.

Ever growing space requirements with an ever growing unused spaces increase the gap between what is available and what is required. Facility Managers face several challenges in convincing the higher management in getting an approval for an additional building or space.

Health and safety:-

Bio-energy company management system always keeps in mind development of a positive health, safety and environment culture through development of policies and procedures and promotion.

They also provide training and monitoring services to the employees and employers which are intended to encourage employees as an integral part of daily operations. All staff, students, visitors, parent/carers would report any health and safety issues promptly to Melissa Leach or Susan Rogers or a senior member of staff in their absence. Health and Safety issues would be discussed and recorded and the relevant agencies would be informed of the concern that has occurred. The Nursery Manager and Deputy Manager also attend the Level 2 Award in Health and Safety in the workplace, Risk Assessment training and Manual Handling Risk Assessment.

Records of training undertaken by staff are kept by the Nursery Manager along with planned dates for future course attendance and refresher courses as needed.

Safety and Security Policy

At Phoenix we aim to make the nursery a safe and secure place for the children, Parent/Carers, Staff and any Visitors who may enter the setting. We aim to make all the children, parent/carers and staff aware of health and safety issues to minimise the hazards and risks to enable them to thrive in a safe and healthy environment.

Melissa and Sue are the members of staff who have undertaken the appropriate training and are responsible for recording risk assessments, updating policies and ensuring others are aware of safety and security issues.

Health and safety policies:-

As a management priority health and safety as an integral part of business

Carried out all activities safe manner

Find hazards and mitigated through formal assessment

Organization fulfil with current health and safety legislation and apply best practice to all its activities

Employees are encouraged to be proactive on health and safety issues

All employees are required to co-operate with organization and their worker in implementing the policy and make sure that their own work is without risk to themselves .

Environment policy:-

improvement in environmental management system by worker training, consultation and involvement in identifying environment impacts etc are the objective of organization.

Environmental impact also analysis in under organization which is involve potential risk of pollution,

Organization always try to cooperation with the applicable local authority and landlords site on relevant issue.

The Company gives due consideration to environmental issues raised by customers and seeks to respond positively to customer-led environmental initiatives.

The Company works closely with those involved in the manufacturing supply chain, in order to achieve best practice in the environmental aspects of material sourcing, product manufacture, disposal and recycling.

All staff, students, visitors, volunteers, Parent/Carers are aware of the location of fire doors and fire exits, and means of escapes from the nursery. Also to know the location of the nearest fire extinguisher and fire alarm call points and instructions for their use. All staff has attended the Universities in house Fire Warden Training. Emergency exit routes are always tidy and free from obstacles. The Fire Siren is tested weekly. The Nursery manager or Deputy Manager to collect the register from the Kitchen. Staff to take responsibility for the children, and to assist them to immediately vacate the nursery, through the safest exit, if possible through the garden and car park.

Our academic experts are ready and waiting to assist with any writing project you may have. From simple essay plans, through to full dissertations, you can guarantee we have a service perfectly matched to your needs.

Risk Assessment

The majority of the activities that are carried out in the Nursery are generally of low risk in nature and do not require being formally assessed. However if we are planning a trip outside the nursery or are carrying out an activity when the child could be at risk, we would carry out a written risk assessment.

Risk assessments are carried out by Sue Rogers and Melissa Leach and all staff will contribute to these documents. The risk assessments would be carried out on activities, the nursery environment, outside environment, manual handling and outings. They are regularly reviewed, working documents they are displayed in each area of the nursery. Should you have any queries or concerns of your own please feel free to talk to Sue or Melissa. Risk assessments are brought to the attention of all relevant staff and students parent/carers and anyone who is involved in the activity. Risk assessments are reviewed annually. Risk assessments are periodically passed to the Health and Safety Department for checking to ensure that they are suitable and sufficient.

Importance of quality to facilities management:-

As a profession facility management used to strategically provide quality working environment. But it required top level management support and accurate requirements defined by consumers. Today current environment of innovation and increasing completion among suppliers, it is imperative for facilities management service provides to implement quality management. Organization gets success through introducing quality management techniques.

That's by productivity can be improved and absenteeism reduced by improving the internal environment.

According to Alexander, "it is a total quality approach to sustaining an operational environment and providing support services to meet the strategic needs of an organization."(1996).

BIBLIOGRAPHY

Alder, Steve. "Disaster and Recovery Planning: A Guide for Facility Managers." Security Management. June 2005.

Brown, Malcolm. "Rulers of the New Frontier." Management Today. March 1996.

Friday, Stormy. Organization Development for Facility Managers. AMACOM, a Division of the American Management Association, 2003.

Huston, John. "Mastering the Facility." Buildings. December 1999.

Kruk, Leonard B. "Facilities Planning Supports Changing Office Technologies." Managing Office Technology. December 1996.

Levitt, Alan M. Disaster Planning and Recovery: A Guide for Facility Professionals. John Wiley & Sons, 1997.

Lewis, Bernard T. and Richard P. Payant. The Facility Manager's Emergency Preparedness Handbook. AMACOM, a Division of the American Management Association, 2003.

O'Brien, Raymond. "Facility Managers Provide Invaluable Services." Managing Office Technology. September 1995.

Price, Steven M. "Facilities Planning: A Perspective for the Information Age." IIE Solutions. August 1997.

Sopko, Sandy. "Smaller Staffs and Budgets Boost FM Outsourcing." The Office. August 1993.

Tuveson, Kit. "Facility Management in the 21st Century." Managing Office Technology. May 1998.

Fm Sourcing & Procurement Influencing Elements

Outsourcing in Facilities Management

While specific facilities services have been strategically sourced since a long time, FM as a function has been considered for outsourcing only in the last few years in view of the profession becoming more mature and complex, and third-party property management companies taking on broader roles. Organizations increasingly recognize the difficulty and cost associated with retaining all of the necessary expertise and technical resources. More companies are turning to single-source providers to manage aspects of their facilities.

Decisions regarding the outsourcing of non-core functions are based on some of the following criteria:

Can we reduce costs and improve services beyond our own capabilities?

Can there be a single point of responsibility for essential support services while maintaining required control?

Are there case examples and documented experiences to ensure that outsourcing is the best mode of service delivery?

The selected facilities service providers need to demonstrate that their performance matches industry standards as well as the metrics of peers and competitors. One of the challenges for outsourcing providers is that once buyer companies experience initial cost benefits through outsourcing, they continue looking for cost savings. They use the new lower cost base as the standard to achieve further reductions, not considering that business costs increase every year.

Operating in an Outsourced Environment

In-house facilities management staff will get directly affected by corporate cost reduction initiatives when transitioned ('rebadged') to an outsourced vendor. The in-house staff will likely receive lower total compensation because FM has traditionally been a low-margin business. This benefits the FM provider initially since transitioned employees have an intimate knowledge of the buyer's culture, mission, or operations environment. Vendors generally agree to retain wage parity for transitioned workers for no longer than six months or a year. Eventually the compensation is reduced to conform to the vendor's own salary structure. Job security is not guaranteed beyond an introductory time period, though employees might find security in the stability of the contract. The vendor, however, wants to be able to let go of employees as quickly as possible so that an outsourced employee's career with the vendor is somewhat reliant on the contract developed for the buyer. If a contract is terminated without renewal, the employee is not guaranteed a new position with another contract.

Balancing Outsourcing and "In-sourcing"

Outsourcing tends to follow cyclical patterns, balancing cost and quality. Companies initially outsource to reduce costs, and then return functions back in-house in order to regain lost service quality.

The benefits of outsourcing include:

Transfer of personnel responsibilities: This important benefit means that once an employee gets sick, the service provider will find a replacement at no added cost. This eliminates the need for the buyer to find a replacement and pay for extra work.

Changing employees that do not perform at agreed upon standards of performance: This is easier to demand from an outsourcing provider.

Possibility of greater learning: From the facility management employee's perspective, large outsourcing companies tend to provide the possibility of greater learning and career progress for functional facility management specialists when in- house organizations don't offer similar opportunities.

The most common down-sides of outsourcing are the normal service quality problems, lost in-house expertise and smaller, de-motivated service staff count. Implications from outsourcing often do not become apparent until the second or third cycle of an outsourcing program, when companies, after several years of outsourcing, realize that they have lost the industry knowledge and ability to competently specify and manage outsourced services.

Trends in Facilities Management

In the face of mounting cost reduction pressures, facilities managers are finding ways to increase efficiencies through:

Higher-quality maintenance at lower cost: Doing more with less by accomplishing objectives with reduced capital expenditure, and less time and people/square foot, they are constantly trying to improve efficiency through better planning and scheduling or including time-saving products for maintenance tasks.

Applying automation technology: Facilities managers are increasing their reliance on hand-held devices to minimize paperwork and boost the accuracy of data collection, the integration of facilities management functions, and increasing their focus on integrating facility/ maintenance/ building control systems.

Outsourcing and the derived benefits of improved personnel training: Facilities managers have access to deeper domain expertise and technology and the ability to better track equipment performance.

Concentrating on core competencies, acquiring expertise: Facilities managers using outside contractors are ultimately able to cut overall facilities management expenses and investments.

New approaches forced upon them by tightened budgets: Facilities managers are forced to squeeze the most functionality out of existing space by creating customized cost-effective and productivity-enhancing facilities to suit the needs of the organization. This is accomplished by conserving energy through energy audits and related improvement programs, employing temporary staff to assist in-house staff with unplanned work, and ensuring facilities run at full capacity all the time.

Future of Facility management

Technology will play an integral role in facility management

Applications in e-sourcing, e-procurement, business planning, and management will help achieve improvements in process effectiveness, monitoring of costs and benefits among several options.

Value creation will gain importance

As facility managers are required to expand their roles and accountabilities, they will gain expertise in project and people management, as well as energy management and productivity measurement to create tangible value for the organization.

Outsourcing partnerships will become the norm

As facility managers include corporate requirements into their operations, they will need to integrate increasing financial considerations to minimize capital risk and outsource non-critical business assets and services.

On conclusion, every organization depends on a combination of resources and services needed to support the core business processes. Make sure that the support is available in the right way. Quality and the right price are the responsibility of facilities management. In essence, took facilities management, and organizations will have the freedom to do what they do best. Operators to take care of the rest. In practice, it has proved difficult to facilities management amplification. British Institute of Facilities Management and the integration of multi-disciplinary " known developments in the built environment and its effects on individuals and work management. Activities and responsibilities and the United Kingdom sector skills council, which hosts more than facilities management is a simple preference in reference to support the integration is necessary for a successful performance. In part, these definitions reserves the right to manage a relatively new idea. Only in the last ten years, most organizations have started to think in terms of strategic importance.

Printed by Libri Plureos GmbH in Hamburg,
Germany